AMERICAN SAILING CRAFT

BOOKS BY HOWARD I. CHAPELLE

Pinky "True Love" of Gloucester, 1815–40   *From a Painting by George Wales*

AMERICAN SAILING CRAFT

by

HOWARD I. CHAPELLE

INTERNATIONAL MARINE PUBLISHING COMPANY
CAMDEN, MAINE

PUBLISHER'S PREFACE

Being a publishing house that specializes in marine books, International Marine naturally fields many questions from readers asking for specific information about specific types of vessels. It works something like guilt-by-association; because we, as publishers, deal with authors who know a great deal about vessels, it is assumed that we ourselves must therefore know all the answers. Regrettably, such is not the case.

In answering such queries, the author we probably turn to most often is Howard I. Chapelle, and one of his most-thumbed books in our office has been *American Sailing Craft*, a highly valuable reference that has been long out of print. The heavy demand for the kinds of information and vessel plans contained in this book convinced us that we should reprint it.

The contents of *American Sailing Craft* first saw print as a series of articles in *Yachting* magazine in the early Thirties. The articles were gathered together and published in book form by Kennedy Brothers, publisher of *Yachting*, in 1936. The book was reprinted by Crown Publishers in 1939, but has been out of print for more than thirty years.

One reason why Howard Chapelle wanted to present to yachtsmen of the Thirties articles on the history and development of such indigenous American working watercraft as the New Haven sharpie, the Cape Cod catboat, and the Friendship sloop was that he felt such craft to be eminently suitable as means to relatively cheap boating in a time of considerable economic hardship. For the same reason, this reprint edition of *American Sailing Craft* would appear to be quite timely.

All his life Howard Chapelle applied his great energy, quick mind, and discerning judgment to researching on, writing about, and drawing plans of the boats and vessels of the past. His chief purpose was to make these records before such primary source ma-

▼

PUBLISHER'S PREFACE

terial as existed during his time might be lost. He pursued this purpose with single-minded industry for over half a century. The result is an unparalleled list of outstanding books of marine history illustrated by hundreds upon hundreds of his own drawings of the craft described.

In reprinting Howard I. Chapelle's *American Sailing Craft*, we are glad to make available again one of his fine contributions to the recording of our maritime heritage. But beyond that, we hope that many readers of this book will gain insight to the satisfactions to be achieved from the building and sailing of the sorts of simple, workable boats and vessels that appear on the following pages.

Roger C. Taylor
International Marine

FOREWORD

THE early history of all maritime nations is largely the story of how the peoples of those countries conquered the sea, and of the ships they built and sailed. Small nations became powerful through their mastery of the sea, through the trade their ships built up, the commerce they controlled and the opportunity for exploration and conquest which the sea that washed their shores offered. Those nations that had the best sailors and built the best ships prospered mightily.

This was as true of the American commonwealth in the colonial days and the years following its birth as a nation as of any other country. More so, perhaps, as owing to its geographical situation it was entirely dependent on the sea for its very existence—for its communication with the mother country, for its intercourse with the other colonies and the West Indies, and for the food and profit that its fisheries produced. The sea was the only highway at its disposal in the early days. Our ancestors became, therefore, a seafaring stock of necessity, even though their roots were buried in rural England.

It is true also that every seafaring nation has developed distinctive types of craft to suit its particular needs. These were governed largely by the nature of the waters in which the vessels were to be used, and by the use to which they were to be put. Thus, a very different form of hull and rig was evolved on a rocky coast with deep water and long, swinging seas than in a country where the waters were shallow and scoured by heavy tides.

In all this development of type and rig, tradition has played an important part. The seaman is by nature conservative. What his forefathers had tried and found good he was slow to abandon. This is not surprising for, after all, one who follows the sea trusts his life to his ship and her gear once he shoves off from shore, and he prefers the known and the tried to the new and untried. Slow development there is, of course, but in that development the effect of one's heritage, of tradition, is always a predominant factor.

It is for this reason that the work done by Howard I. Chapelle in preserving for posterity the early American types of boats that were the ancestors of those in which we sail today is of such great value to the yachtsman and to those who love the sea and ships. In this book he has confined himself to the smaller craft that were used alongshore and coastwise, with occasional voyages to the Maritime Provinces of Nova Scotia and to the West Indies, because these were more distinctly American in type, and their development was in accordance with our particular needs. They are all typical of what some geographical section of our varied coastline or some special service demanded. Such, for instance, as the Friendship sloop, indigenous to the rocky coast of Maine with its deep water and its hard winter gales; or the Gloucester fishing fleet, from the first pinkies to the beautiful schooners of the early years of this century; or the shoal centerboarders that the shallow waters south of Cape Cod and in the Bay of the Chesapeake demanded. The chapters dealing with the American pilot boat as developed from Norfolk, Virginia, to Boston are of intense interest to yachtsmen, for it was from one of these boats that the yacht *America* was born, whose existence and achievements had a profound effect on the development of yachting in the United States. All of the types described are known by name and fame to those whose interest today lies on the water, yet but few of the original craft still survive and to many persons they are but names. Mr. Chapelle has rendered the present generation, and those still to come, a service beyond reward in preserving the lines, the method of construction and the history of these craft.

In getting his material together the author has spent years of research and study. In some cases he was lucky enough to find an existing example of the type he wanted and from her was able to take off the lines; but even then he had to go still further back, to that boat's forebears, to note changes from the original that time had wrought in this last of her line. Much of the information sought was found in dusty half-models unearthed from old shipyards or

FOREWORD

from the descendants of those who owned and sailed these early vessels, or from records kept by marine societies and associations of master mariners. But, wherever it came from, the information he unearthed and has here passed on is authentic. Except for this record it might well have happened that many of the types here preserved on paper would have become lost in obscurity of an age careless of records and with the passing of those who actually knew and remembered the boats as they were.

Not only to those interested in tracing the development of small boat types will this story of American Sailing Craft appeal. For Mr. Chapelle both feels and sees the romance, the struggle, the brave endeavor lying back of that early fleet that served the people of the United States — at that time scattered in a fringe along the Atlantic seaboard — aand helped to make them the nation they are today. What is more, he makes the reader see and feel it also.

HERBERT L. STONE

New York, N. Y.
May 5, 1936

PREFACE

THERE were over a hundred types of American sailing craft employed in the fisheries and in commerce between 1800 and 1900. A few scattered pictures, half-models and plans are all that remain of many of these types — some have left only their names. The few types now "alive" are gradually disappearing. It seems important, therefore, that records be made of every type possible before it is too late.

The late Martin Erismann began the work of recording vanishing American sailing craft early in the present century but, unfortunately, his untimely death put a period to his labors before he had succeeded in describing more than a few scattered types. This book is intended to carry on the work he so ably began.

Aside from the recording of these old types, I have the desire to show the possibilities of building yachts to meet the special requirement of employment and local geographical conditions as compared to the limitations imposed by the conventional yacht types now in use.

For their generous assistance in obtaining information, I wish to express my obligation to M. V. Brewington, Jr.; Lewis H. Story; C. Knight, former Curator of the Admiralty; H. Richardson, Admiralty Curator; W. D. McLean, of John McLean & Sons, Ltd.; H. Manley Crosby; W. C. McKay & Sons, Ltd.; The Bureau of Construction and Repair, U. S. N. Dept.; Frank A. Taylor, Curator, Division of Engineering, U. S. National Museum; Captain Charlton L. Smith; W. P. Stephens; Lawrence A. Jenkins, Curator, Peabody Marine Museum; David Foster Taylor; Charles G. Davis; George C. Wales; Charles H. Hall; Charles M. Blackford; The Rudder Publishing Co.; and Thomas F. MacManus.

Among the sources consulted for data were the following: *The Commodore's Story,* Ralph M. Munroe and Vincent Gilpin, Ives Washburn, 1930; *Report on Shipbuilding,* Hall, 10th U. S. Census; *History of the Fore and Aft Rig in America,* E. P. Morris, Yale

PREFACE

Press; *Architectura Mercatoria Navalis,* Chapman, 1763; *Manual of Yacht and Boat Sailing,* Dixon Kemp, Horace Cox, 4th edition, London, 1884; *From Sandy Hook to 62°,* Charles E. Russell, The Century Co., New York, 1929; *Marine and Naval Architecture,* John Willis Griffiths, George Philip & Sons, London, 1857; *The Opium Clippers,* Basil Lubbock, Brown, Son & Ferguson, Glasgow, 1933; *Plans of Wooden Ships,* Wm. Webb, New York; *Reports of the U. S. Fish Commission,* Government Printing Office; *Catalogue of the Watercraft Collection in the U. S. National Museum,* Carl W. Mitman, Government Printing Office, 1923; *Yachting,* Kennedy Brothers, Inc., New York; *The Rudder,* Rudder Publishing Co., New York; *Ships of the Past,* Charles G. Davis, Marine Research Society, Salem, Mass., 1929.

HOWARD IRVING CHAPELLE

Scituate, Mass.
April 14, 1936

TABLE OF CONTENTS

Chapter One

⚓

THE NEW HAVEN SHARPIE

Chapter One

⚓

THE NEW HAVEN SHARPIE

Many yachtsmen speak longingly of "cheap yachts," without appreciating the true inference of the term. The actual cost of a "cheap" yacht will vary, of course, with the individual, but such a yacht must be "the most boat for the money." There are but two possible ways of building an inexpensive sailing yacht. One is to find a builder foolish enough to present you with a boat at a price below cost, or one who, by means of low labor costs and suitable location, can afford to build at a low figure. In such cases, a yacht of more or less orthodox type is possible, but frequently at the sacrifice of workmanship, finish and appearance. The other possibility is the use of a hull type whose form is such that little labor and inexpensive materials are required.

Either of these procedures may result in a cheap and useful yacht for ordinary work. There is a good deal of "bunk" about the necessity of seaworthiness, and though numerous yachts suitable for riding out a winter gale on the Grand Banks are designed and built, yet their actual cruising is limited to protected water and to short 'longshore jumps in good weather. If, for business reasons or by inclination, one cruises under such conditions, it would seem poor judgment to demand a real seagoing yacht and to pay the required price.

To those who admit to themselves that their cruising is thus limited, the sharpie offers a cheap and rather satisfactory type. Some forty or fifty years ago the sharpie was popular as a yacht, but disappeared when the racing machines of the "length and sail area" period became popular. As a matter of fact, the sharpie was directly

3

responsible for the scow type, and from the sharpie developed the extreme rating classes of the early 1900's.

It is impossible to say when the sharpie first came into use. Probably in the 1830's or 40's the New Haven oystermen found that the cost of the dugout canoes then in use was becoming prohibitive and began to use the ordinary flat-bottom skiff, fitted with a centerboard and leg-of-mutton sail. By 1857, the sharpie had begun to develop from the sailing skiff, and two-masted rigs were in use. The sharpie of 1870 was small, its length being between 20 and 28 feet in the majority of boats. About 1878, an Englishman named Thomas Clapham became interested in the type and began building sharpies at Roslyn, Long Island. He developed a modified type known as the nonpareil, or Roslyn type, which had a little deadrise in the extreme bow and stern, the bottom remaining flat amidships. Many of the Clapham sharpies were yawl-rigged and most of them were built for yachting purposes. The leading New Haven builder was Lester Rowe, whose boats were all true sharpies and who is said to have turned out the fastest one ever built. Most of the New Haven builders turned out commercial craft only.

Oddly enough the sharpie as a yacht became popular abroad before it became so at home. During the early seventies a Frenchman named More made two visits to Long Island Sound, each time taking home a small sharpie, the second being a small nonpareil sharpie. These two boats were the subject of much attention abroad and their speed resulted in many yachts being built on their lines. As a matter of fact, the French government built some 40-foot sharpies, armed with a small revolving cannon on top of the house, for use as patrol boats in the colonies. These were exact copies of the New Haven sharpies of the eighties, except for increased beam and displacement. Even the peculiar rig of this date was duplicated in these patrol boats.

Eventually, the Americans became interested, the controversy between keel and centerboard adherents having caused a widespread interest in new types. During the eighties and nineties the sharpie yacht became very common, usually, however, in more or less modified form. A number of the sharpie yachts were rather large, many being of the Clapham type, rigged as yawls or schooners.

During the nineties Larry Huntington began experimenting with sharpies, building them on Long Island, and he, too, developed a modified type. Where Clapham had employed straight deadrise, which soon evolved into the skipjack or V-bottom, Huntington

A NEW HAVEN SHARPIE

used a rounded bottom athwartships, retaining the flat sides and chines of the orthodox sharpie. The Huntington type remained a true sharpie, except for the slight camber in the bottom athwartships. Usually this was an arc of a circle amidships, the amount of camber being quite small there and decreasing towards bow and stern. This feature increased the speed in light airs. After the half-rater *Question "cleaned up"* on the Sound the Huntington type was widely copied. The *Question* marked the coming of the scow, and both Huntington and Clapham had a part in the development of this type.

5

In the meantime the use of the sharpie had spread with the oyster business from Long Island Sound to the Chesapeake, the Carolina sounds, and to Florida. Later, it was used in the West

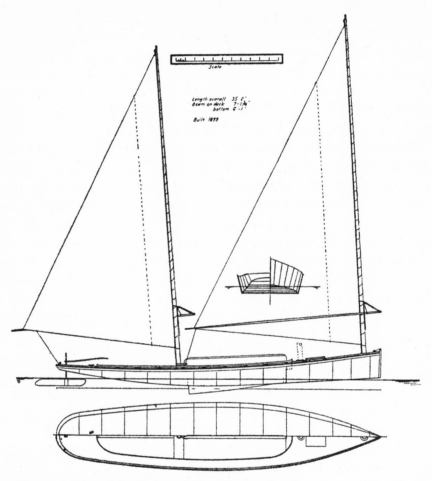

Figure 1. Lines and sail plan of New Haven sharpie built by Lester Rowe, a well-known builder of sharpies

Indies and on the Great Lakes. There is no other type of small boat that has spread as rapidly and as far as the sharpie. R. M. Munroe introduced the type into Florida waters in the 1870's, and his well known *Egret*, a double-ender, is described in *The Commodore's*

Story. This boat was probably the best seagoing sharpie type yet evolved. Most of the commercial sharpies in Florida waters were schooner-rigged, while on the Carolina sounds the New Haven hull and rig remained unchanged for many years. Eventually, the Carolina builders adopted the schooner rig, but retained the New Haven hull with the straight, upright stem. The Florida sharpies generally used clipper stems. While the gaff rig was occasionally employed, the leg-of-mutton was the most common. The sharpie has had many uses, having been gainfully employed as oyster boat, sponger, mail boat, cargo boat, Spanish mackerel fisherman, Cuban gun-runner, and, more lately, even as a "bootie."

Obviously, the sharpie had excellent qualities to bring it into such widespread use and to have outlived so many other types. Hence the type seems worthy of careful attention. In 1928 the lines of a New Haven, or Fairhaven, sharpie, Figure 1, one of the last and best of Lester Rowe's sharpies, and chosen by his son, were taken off. The two-masted rig is rarely seen now, even in New Haven. The fore-mast is usually placed in the middle step, just forward of the center-board case, and the boat is steered with an oar in place of the rudder. With this rig a crew of one is all that is required, though two or more men were formerly employed in each boat when oystering.

Figure 1 shows the sharpie in its best form, as an oyster boat. In size, the New Haven sharpies are about 35 feet long, though they have been built up to lengths of 60 feet or more. An old oysterman told me that a 60-foot sharpie, with three masts, had been built on Long Island in the early nineties for Carolina owners. She was lost through collision on her way south. As described, she was 60 feet over all, 9'-10" extreme beam, and was flush-decked. She had a cuddy forward, and a low house aft; she steered with a wheel and had a regular sharpie rig, except that she had three masts. The mainmast was tallest, the foremast next in height, and the mizzen was shortest of all. The mainmast was 48 feet long, there being a short club on each sprit. It was claimed that this sharpie was extraordinarily fast on the wind.

Several 60-foot sharpie yachts that showed great speed have been built. Usually they had schooner or yawl rigs and were of the nonpareil type. A 40-footer is reported to have made 14 knots under favorable conditions, for a number of hours.

The faults of many sharpie yachts lay in in disregard of the requirements of this particular hull form. As in the case of so many types, to design a sharpie properly demands a knowledge of its peculiarities. There are certain fixed rules in sharpie design and these can be broken only under certain conditions, which are met in the modified types only. It should be remembered that most boat types are developed by means of trial and error, over a period of years, hence modification must be made only after considerable study of the type. In the sharpie this is markedly true; seventy years of continuous evolution cannot be disregarded with impunity.

The rules for sharpie proportions and form are approximately as follows:

1. The beam on the bottom should be about 1/6th the over all length.

2. The flare amidships should be 3½ inches to 4 inches per foot of depth — less if speed alone is desired, more if seaworthiness and safety are the important factors.

3. The freeboard should be low, but a rather strong sheer is highly desirable.

4. The displacement must be as light as possible, with the usual sharpie construction; outside ballast, heavy keels, and heavy displacement must be avoided.

5. The chine line, in elevation, must appear as follows: the heel of the stem should be above the water line; the chine runs straight for about one-third the over all length of the hull abaft the stem, sloping downwards toward the midsection. The chine then curves gently to the point of greatest draft, and runs upward to the stern in a flat, gentle curve. A long run is important.

6. A light rig is necessary for safety. Due to the narrow beam and lack of ballast, the multiple-masted rigs with low centers of effort are best; one-masted sharpies, of the proper proportions of hull, are not sufficiently canvased for high speed in light airs.

For the best results in the sharpie type the hull weights and spars should be light.

If it is desirable, because of accommodation or rig requirements, to increase the beam, some deadrise, at least in the run, is necessary. This was done in the Chesapeake variation of the sharpie, the

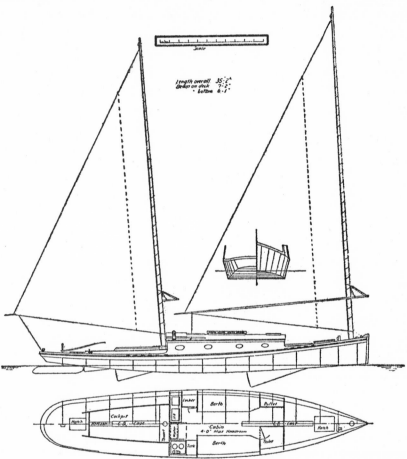

Figure 2. A sharpie yacht

Hampton flattie. Clapham introduced deadrise at both bow and stern in order to employ a larger displacement and more beam than is permissible in the pure New Haven type. It is commonly supposed that deadrise in bow and stern will prevent pounding; however, this is not the case in any of the sharpie or skipjack types.

While the sharpie will pound only when upright, the skipjack, if given enough deadrise to prevent this, will pound when heeled. The Chesapeake skipjack has little deadrise, and is sailed on her chine,

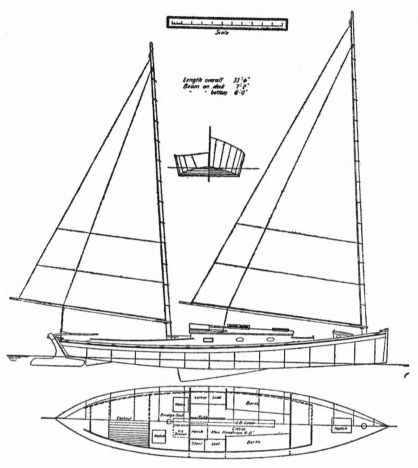

Figure 3. A 33-foot sharpie for yacht use

like the New Haven sharpie, as the builders have found that a dead-rise of over 25 degrees to the horizontal hurts the sailing qualities of the type. All modifications of the sharpie are more expensive to build than the parent type, and it is doubtful whether the extra cost is warranted in most cases, though in large sizes the nonpareil type

permits the greatest accommodation. The excuse for either nonpareil or flattie is the increase in the displacement permissible,
wihtout an increase in length.

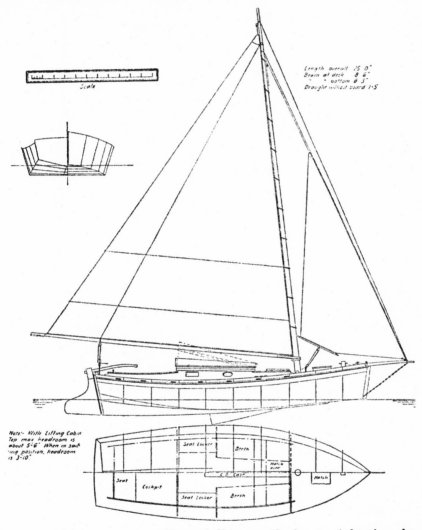

Figure 4. Hampton flattie type of sharpie yacht

The two-masted rig, shown in Figure 1, is typical. The masts have
no shrouds or stays. The diameters of the masts are: at partners,
6 inches; at head, 1½ inches. The sprit is supported at the heel by a

snotter and tackle. A single block, fitted with a side shackle and becket, is strapped to the mast; the snotter is a pennant with an eye spliced into one end, the sprit passing through the eye. This is also fastened to the mast by the same strap as the block. The tackle is spliced to the becket on the block and rove through a slot or hole in the heel of the sprit, then back through the block, belaying to a cleat on the mast.

The masts must revolve in their steps and there is usually a brass plate fastened to the heel of each mast, another being placed in each step; these act as bearings. The sails are reefed parallel to the masts, the sails being lowered to tie in the reefs. In the old rig there was a

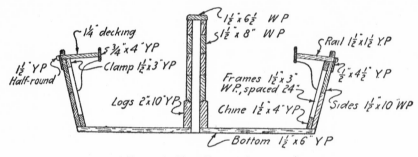

Typical New Haven Construction

vertical batten which was hauled to the mast by brails instead of reef points.

Sharpies usually have no skegs, and use balance rudders, which are fitted to lift by fixing a pin in the stock at the desired depth. The centerboard must be very long, which is an objection, as it invariably cuts up the cabin arrangement. Two smaller boards can be used, if desired. In length the single board should be equal to about one-third of the over all length of the hull. In this 35-foot sharpie, the centerboard is 10'-4" long, about 3'-0" wide, and 2 inches thick.

The construction is very simple. The backbone consists of the long centerboard case, and a log keelson aft. This is made of three 2" x 8" timbers on edge, tapered aft. The sides are wide planks; usually three or four strakes are used. There is no rabbet on the stem, the planks being fastened to a triangular stem piece, and beveled together, the whole being covered by a brass plate serving as a cut-water. The stern, if square, is set with a strong rake; if round, as in the boat shown, it is stayed vertically with narrow stuff, on two

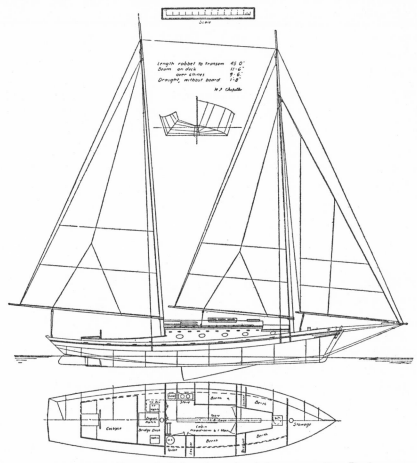

Figure 5. A sharpie yacht of the nonpareil or Roslyn type

stern frames. The bottom is always cross-planked, fastened to the sides and to chine logs as well. A sheer clamp is employed, cleats taking the place of frames. Oyster boats have but one bulkhead, just forward of the centerboard case. Stock of 1½ inches is used throughout, mostly white pine; as a rule, the bottom is of yellow pine.

The sharpie yachts shown in Figures 2, 3, 4 and 5 were based on the sharpie in Figure 1. Holding very closely to the original, Figure 2 shows a yacht of the New Haven type. The only changes were in the stern, which was deepened, and the displacement had to be increased to bear the extra weight of cabin, house and fittings. Double centerboards are used to permit a comfortable cabin arrangement, entailing some extra cost. A small skeg is shown but this can be omitted if weeds are not often encountered. This sharpie should be quite fast, and is suitable for protected waters. Her headroom is about the maximum for this length, 4'-0".

Figure 3 shows a more seagoing type. She is based on Commodore R. M. Munroe's fine old double-ender *Egret,* and is designed along lines suggested by him. She is suitable for a single-hander and for beaching, and is as simple as possible .Her sails are fitted with booms, but no standing rigging is required. A berth can be fitted in the fore peak. This sharpie is on New Haven proportions, but the round stern is replaced by a sharp one. The skeg can be omitted, if desired, and an inboard rudder post, as in Figure 2, can be used. Her headroom is also 4'-0".

It does not seem practical to design a cabin sharpie under 28 feet over all on New Haven proportions, as the narrow beam and the space required by the centerboard do not permit much in the way of accommodations. Hence, when a small sharpie is wanted, something similar to Figure 4 is the result. The deadrise aft is necessary to clear the run. In this example an attempt is made to retain the sailing qualities of the Hampton flattie. The lifting cabin top is similar to that shown in Cook's *Single-Handed Sailing.* No shrouds are used on the mast, unless desired. Construction is the same as in the New Haven sharpie, except for the slight deadrise aft. Deadrise is not introduced to prevent pounding but to reduce wetted surface, which, with excess stability, are the chief causes of failure in the wide sharpies.

Figure 5 shows a nonpareil sharpie with a leg-of-mutton schooner rig, 45 feet long. She is about the minimum length in which full headroom can be expected. A small amount of deadrise fore and aft has been employed, after Clapham's method, to permit an increase in displacement which otherwise could not be used with the flat bottom. This design is particularly suitable for Florida waters. Small ventilators are shown over the ports in the trunk. This boat is seaworthy enough to make any necessary outside jumps in good weather.

It is not claimed that this type is suitable for extended cruising in blue water. However, comparatively few of us are in a position to take long voyages, so possibly the sharpie will meet the needs of many boat sailors. For those living on tidal waters where harbors dry out at low tide, the sharpie is an excellent type. It will serve with safety and satisfaction in all localities where the water is shoal.

Pounding, when upright at anchor, is a fault of all sharpies. It was the custom to run small cruising sharpies on a mud or sand bank, or to beach them for the night, to avoid this annoyance. It is usually possible to get large sharpies into a smooth anchorage, as they draw so little water. Some pounding must be expected underway, of course.

In the drawings no attempt has been made to "pretty up" the type; it is possible to use curved stems, for example, but the only result is a useless increase in cost. If curved stems are employed, some curvature in the sides, at least forward, is required, which serves no useful purpose.

The two-masted sharpie, of the New Haven type, is sailed like a centerboard sloop with a large jib, the foresail taking the place of the jib. In strong breezes it is best to ease a sharpie by slacking the fore sheet, rather than by the sudden easing of the helm, as the stern slews around so fast on the helm that water may come aboard or the boat may trip and capsize. In careful hands there is no danger, however. Heavy rigs, well stayed, make the small sharpie unsafe. The working sharpies will be dismasted before they can capsize, which is one of the reasons why no shrouds are used. Their light, limber spars permit the wind to spill out when the boat is heavily pressed. The whip of these spars seems to help their sailing, as is the case with so many light hulls. Certainly, they can carry their sail longer when the masts are unstayed.

The chief recommendations of the sharpie are its cheapness, speed and ease of handling. It is possible that some readers may find in this type a boat suitable for their needs. At least, the sharpie is a most interesting craft, and the present generation of yachtsmen should be acquainted with its qualities.

Chapter Two

⚓

THE SKIPJACK

Chapter Two

⚓

THE SKIPJACK

THE most popular hull form for cheap sailing yachts is the V-bottom, sometimes known as the "diamond-bottom," but more widely called the "skipjack." This type of hull is a direct descendant of the sharpie, and has some similarity in design. The skipjack is a natural development of the old nonpareil sharpies of the early eighties, and was developed to permit the use of greater displacement than was desirable in the nonpareil type of hull. The V-bottom hull had a limited popularity on Long Island Sound, particularly in the vicinity of New London, Conn., in the eighties. Clapham had developed this type at the conclusion of the evolution of the nonpareil sharpie. Why the type is called "skipjack" is not evident, but the name was applied very early in its development.

It was on Chesapeake Bay, however, that the skipjack was most highly developed, and where it enjoyed the greatest popularity. The Chesapeake skipjack has always been given a fine reputation for speed and weatherliness, and is one of the most striking and distinctive of American small sailing boat types. The history of the type is still incomplete, but such evidence as could be found makes the following seem fairly accurate.

The New Haven type of sharpie was employed in the oyster business on the Bay in the early days, and it is possible that these boat were introduced from the Sound about 1868. However, the sharpie, while still used on the Bay, was never a very popular type there. The reason for this was that the distances to market on the Bay were greater, requiring a larger and more burdensome boat than was necessary on the Sound.

AMERICAN SAILING CRAFT

Except for this situation, the weather and water conditions on the Bay are like those on the Sound. Both bodies of water can be very rough and uncomfortable, and both are very shoal in places, particularly on the oyster beds. Thus the demand for light draft boats existed in both places. However, the Bay oystermen appear to have had a preference for the sloop rig in the early days; even in the log canoes this rig was popular.

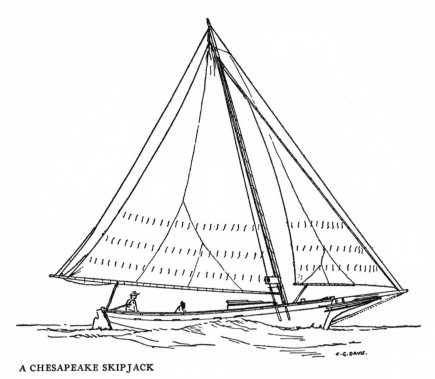

A CHESAPEAKE SKIPJACK

At any rate, the early sloop-rigged and beamy sharpies on the Bay were given a little deadrise aft, to make them sail better, and this type became known as Hampton flatties. Their rig was that of a gaff-rigged sloop, without a bowsprit. These boats were rarely over 30 feet in length, and had no cabin. Another type was also developed; these were called "bateaux," and were small, narrow, flat-bottomed boats, leg-of-mutton sloop rigged; they were open boats, and most of them were double-enders. As the necessity for

larger and more burdensome boats increased, the development
of the skipjack from the Hampton flattie was inevitable. This im-

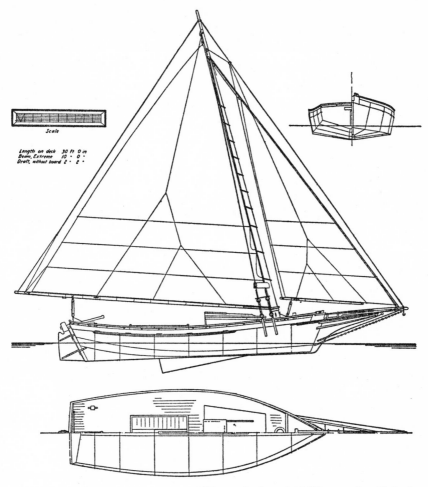

Figure 6. *A typical Chesapeake skipjack,*
the lines being taken from an existing boat

provement must have taken place sometime in the early nineties,
though the skipjack is not mentioned in print until much later.

Skipjack yachts have been popular, not only with amateur designers and builders, but with professionals. The famous yawl, *Sea*

Bird, in which Thomas Day crossed the Atlantic, is one of the best known of skipjack yachts, but she differs greatly from the Chesapeake model. Day's report on her qualities, as well as later reports on copies built on her lines, show that pounding was not wholly overcome; it is apparently impossible to avoid this fault in the V-bottom hull. It seems likely that the seaworthiness of the model has been somewhat overrated. However, the Bay skipjack has many excellent features and has been quite successful, while V-bottom sailing yachts have not been uniformly satisfactory. Many such yachts are slow and do not carry their sail as well as could be desired. A study of two fast sailing Chesapeake skipjacks seems to show the reasons for the lack of success of the V-bottom in yachts.

The skipjacks on the Bay vary in length from 28 to 60 feet, but all are built on the same rule of thumb proportions. The lines of two examples were taken off, one 38′ x 13′ x 4′; the other, 30′ x 10′ x 2′-2″. Both were on a similar model, differing only in minor details. The larger boat had been built about 1898 for the oyster business; the smaller boat, of about the same date of build, was a farmer's boat. Because of their similarity, only the smaller skipjack is illustrated in Figure 6.

Through the kindness of M. V. Brewington, Jr., the Bay rules for building skipjacks are available. They are as follows: The greatest beam is one-third of the length on deck, and is located between one-half and two-thirds of the length on deck abaft the stem. The width of the transom is about three-quarters of the greatest beam. The flare of the sides varies from 2 inches to 3 inches for each foot of depth amidships, according to the practice of the builder. The mast step is located one-fifth or one-sixth of the length on the water line, abaft the stem, varying somewhat with the size of the boat, and the mast rakes about 75 degrees to the l.w.l., the masthead coming directly over the point of greatest beam. The length of the mast is equal to the length on deck, plus the greatest beam. The length of the bowsprit, outboard, is equal to the greatest beam. The length of the boom is equal to the length of the hull on deck. The length of the centerboard is one-third the length on deck, and is placed in the middle third of the aforementioned length; the board does not appear above the deck.

Figure 6 shows the peculiarities of the type. Attention is called to the following points: The chine, in side elevation, shows the same amount of straightness in the forward end as was seen in the sharpie. The rabbet of the bottom is a curve of the same character as the chine, and the run is long and flat; the deadrise is always small amidships. The chine is always submerged amidships and at the stem. The freeboard is alway low amidships, but there is a strong sheer, which gives high ends, particularly forward. The low free-board, sweeping sheer, and long cutwater, combined, give a very graceful appearance to the hull.

The long cutwater and the head rails are typical of nearly all of the Bay types, but the reason for them is not apparent, though the upper, or head rail, is useful as a place on which to stand when furl-ing the jib. The bowsprit is secured by one or two gammoning irons, and by the characteristic knight-heads, as well as by the bitts. The stern varies; some boats have a transom, as in the figure, while oth-ers have overhang and an inboard rudder. Most of the skipjacks steer with a wheel, except in the smaller boats. In any case, the stem and transom are set with a strong rake, which seems to vary as the flare of the sides. If the stern has overhang, the quarters are quite thin, due to the height of the chine at the tern.

The open rails, supported by short pipe stanchions, through which bolts pass, are common. Like the sharpies, the skipjacks load aft, and so trim by the stern. The center of buoyancy is about amid-ships. The hull, 6 inches above and below the l.w.l., is sheathed with galvanized sheet steel, as ice protection. The centerboard is of the usual type; there is no special gear or construction. The lanyard is made fast to the case in the main hatch, as a rule. The pin is high in the case; the case supports the deck amidships, where the dredge winch is located in an oyster boat.

The deck arrangement varies in accordance with the size of the boat and the trade in which she is employed. The house is most commonly forward, and usually contains two berths and a stove. There is often a wooden horse for the jib sheet, and sometimes one for the main sheet, too. A large main hatch, about amidships, is sometimes accompanied by a small hatch aft; if the house is aft, the small hatch is placed forward, of course.

Few skipjacks have more than two men as crew, and are often sailed single-handed; hence their rig is very simple and rather light. There are some peculiar features in it which are worth attention. The mast is of large diameter at the deck and tapers to a small head; it is supported by two shrouds on each side, set up with lan-

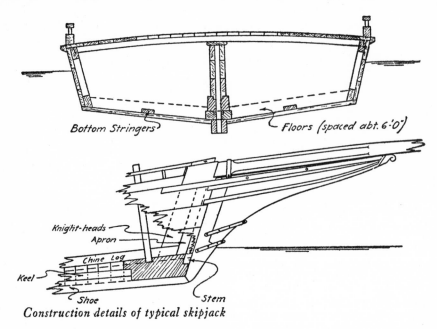

Construction details of typical skipjack

yards. The shrouds are quite slack, which allows the rig to be rather flexible. There are also two stays, a jibstay and a stay to the mast-head. Both lead to the bowsprit; the jibstay, which, like the shrouds, does not run all the way to the masthead, passes through the bow-sprit and thence to the cutwater. The masthead stay leads from a mast band aloft to another band on the bowsprit, to which the two bowsprit shrouds and a chain bobstay are also attached. The shrouds and stays are all of galvanized rigging wire. It is usual to take up the lack in the stays by hogging down the bowsprit with the chain bobstay and jibstay turnbuckles. The hook at the end of the bowsprit serves as a fairlead for the anchor cable to clear the head gear and to prevent chafe. While this must bring a heavy strain on the bowsprit, it appears to do no harm. There is nothing unusual in the mainsail or jib, except that the head of the mainsail sets flying, and a peculiar fitting of the lazy-jacks of the jib. These are attached to a spectacle ring, which rides on the masthead stay, and are raised or lowered with a halliard attached to the ring and reeving through a cheek block on the mast. A similar rig is occasionally used on the mainsail, the ring riding on the toppinglift which in such case is of wire. The idea of this rig is to prevent fouling when the sails are being hoisted. The jib is fitted with a downhaul reeving through a cheek block on the bowsprit, and the mainsail is fitted with a reefing tackle which reeves through a cheek block on the boom in the usual manner. The main boom toppinglift is made fast aloft, with a thimble in the lower end, through which a lanyard is rove. This passes through a cheek block on the boom.

The reason for the extreme rake of the mast is hard to discover. Probably, it is a matter of custom. It possesses two practical advantage, however, which seem to have importance. The first is that it permits the mast to be placed well forward, giving more usable deck space, which would otherwise be impossible in a leg-of-mutton sloop without the use of a tremendously long main boom. The other reason was discovered when calculating the center of effort; the center moved forward very little when the sails were reefed. Were the mast vertical, the movment of the center of effort forward would be great, and while this would not be a serious fault in a narrow boat, in a wide vessel it would cause excessive lee helm, and therefore hard steering. This quality is sometimes observed in beamy yachts with the so-called "modern" jib-headed rig, when reefed down in strong winds, for this same reason. On the whole, the skipjack rig is an efficient one, considering area and cost.

The handling of the skipjack is an important matter. They are sailed well heeled to put them on their chine, whenever possible, so as to prevent pounding in rough water. It is only when upright or when running on their chines that the skipjack model does not pound. It is obvious that, at certain angles of heel, the hull is riding on a flat bottom, and pounding therefore is unavoidable in all V-bottom sailing hulls. The two advantages that the skipjack has over the sharpie are the eliminating of pounding when upright,

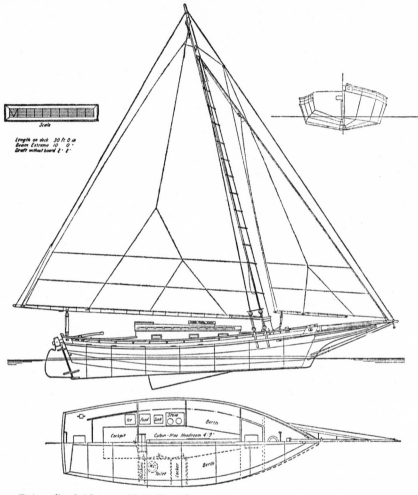

Figure 7. A 30-foot skipjack yacht

particularly at anchor, and the possibility of employing greater displacement.

The construction of the skipjack is marked by economy in labor, materials and cost. In general, the construction of the skipjack is similar to that of the sharpie; the sides are strengthened by sheer battens and chine logs, the strakes are held together by cleats closely spaced, extending from sheer batten to chine log. The bottom is

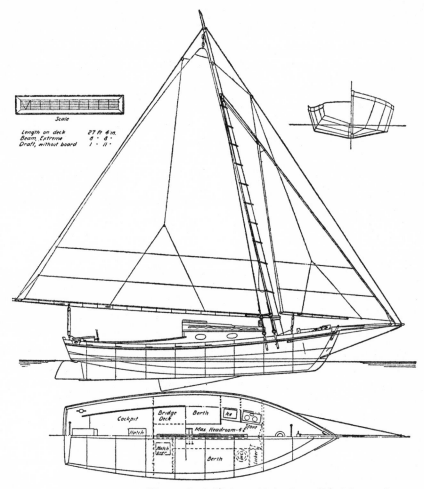

Figure 8. A 27-foot skipjack modified for yacht use

cross-planked. In old boats the planks are laid on at right angles to the keel, but in later boats the planks are laid at an angle of about 45 degrees, sloping aft. The keel is in two parts, a keelson and a shoe. There is no rabbet cut in the keel; the top of the shoe and under side of the keelson are beveled, as shown in the sketch of the midsection. The transom is well kneed to the keelson and to the sides. The stem and forefoot are constructed in the same manner as was done in the old nonpareil sharpie. The keelson and shoe are let into the solid block of timber, forming the forefoot from below; the stem is notched into the fore. end. The forefoot, made up of one or more balks of timber bolted together, is hewn to the required shape and fastened to the chine logs. In some boats the stem is rabbeted, in others an apron is used; the knight-heads serve to secure the fore end of the side strakes, and the sheer battens and the chine log are let into them. The bitt, and often the mast, are stepped into the forefoot timber. The sketch of the stem shows the common construction used in the forefoot.

The Chesapeake shipjacks are of heavy scantling. Yellow pine is generally employed in their construction. The workmanship is rough but strong; the skipjack shows to good advantage when compared with most small fishing and commercial craft.

Two-masted skipjacks, built on bugeye proportions and rig, are successful on the Bay; some are double-ended. Skipjack schooners are sometimes seen in southern waters, but have never been very popular.

Two examples of yacht skipjacks have been worked out to see what was possible in a small boat. The typical rig was adhered to as it seems to answer the requirement of the boats. Figure 7 shows a design following very closely the original type, the freeboard being slightly increased and a long house employed, having a maximum headroom of about 4'-9". A shorter trunk would look better, but room would be sacrificed below. The centerboard case is an obstruction in the cabin that is hard to overcome in this type.

Figure 8 is a modified design with a little curvature worked into the sections forward and into the stem. This boat, while lacking in headroom, would make a useful single-hander and week-end cruiser. The possibilities are far from being exhausted; some very interesting designs could be worked out around the original idea.

The type just described is a highly useful one for shoal waters if more room is necessary than is obtainable in a sharpie. The cost will be greater than that of a sharpie of the same length, but less than that of a round-bottom sailing yacht of the same dimensions. Of course, it is possible to make the skipjack very expensive by unnecessary structural "improvements." Too little attention has been given the cost and necessity of many constructural fads favored in yachts, which is one of the reasons for their high cost.

Chapter Three

⚓

THE FRIENDSHIP SLOOP

⚓

THE FRIENDSHIP SLOOP

THERE has been a good deal of talk about the weatherliness of small sailing yachts and about their ability to claw off a lee shore in a gale. However, there is not one small yacht in ten that can work to windward in really heavy weather. This sounds like a serious indictment; yet it is not, as few yachts are ever under the necessity of sailing to windward in winds of near gale force, since severe summer gales are rare.

Many yachtsmen are under the impression that a narrow, deep yacht, of heavy displacement, and with a lot of outside ballast, must be very weatherly and able to claw off the much discussed lee shore. This is not quite the case, as weatherliness depends not only upon weight and depth, but, of greater importance, upon the ability of the yacht to carry her sail and to stand up under it. A vessel that sails at a great angle of heel in strong winds will not be able to thrash out to windward in a real breeze. The ability of a yacht to stand up under a press of sail in heavy going depends, to a great extent, upon the relationship of the initial stability of the hull to the area of sail carried.

Practically all deep, narrow hulls have little initial stability, regardless of the quantity of ballast outside; hence their power to carry sail in a breeze is much reduced. The importance of outside ballast in cruising yachts for giving stability and power to carry sail is much over-rated, as such ballast does not become efficacious until the vessel is well heeled, and then the efficiency of both sail area and lateral plane are reduced. The necessity of retaining all the efficincy possible in the lateral plane is understood when the strength

33

of the surface drift in a gale, with its leeward scend, is considered.

A practical example of the lack of weatherliness of deep, narrow types are the numerous defeats, during the eighties, of the old, narrow English cutters by wide centerboarders in heavy weather. In spite of their greater displacement and depth, the six-beam cutters could not weather the more powerful centerboarders in strong winds.

In the type which is the subject of this chapter, we shall see the practical use of power to carry sail in heavy weather in order to obtain weatherliness under hard conditions. This ability is secured in a comparatively cheap boat. Power to carry sail and initial stability can be obtained by beam, hardbilges, flaring sides, length, or by combining any two or all these features of design. In the Friendship sloop, we find a combination of these features in a keel sloop. The advantages and disadvantages of great power and weatherliness, as here exemplified, will be easily seen.

To understand the whys and wherefores of the Friendship sloop, it is necessary to know what the boats were used for, and the weather that they had to be prepared to meet. Now, the town of Friendship, as most readers know, is on the coast of Maine; fishing was formerly the chief industry of its inhabitants. In early days, canoes, small sail and rowboats, and later small centerboard sloops, were used in the shore fishing then carried on. The centerboard sloops were introduced some time in the 1850's and were known as "Muscongus Bay boats." They were very popular with the lobstermen. These sloops looked very much like the present Friendship sloop above the load line, but were much shoaler boats. They were usually about 26 feet long; 8 feet beam; and $2\frac{1}{4}$ feet draft, with board raised. The rig was usually that of a single-headsail sloop. The mast was about 26 feet long above the deck; bowsprit, 6 feet outboard; boom, 26 feet long; and gaff, 15 feet long. They were fast, handy and seaworthy craft, and would work under mainsail alone. There is a rigged model of one of these sloops in the Watercraft Collection in the U. S. National Museum at Washington, D. C. These Muscongus Bay sloops were built all along the shore, but the greater number were put up at or in the vicinity of Friendship, by a family of boat-builders named Morse. Some sloops of the Muscongus Bay type were built up to the beginning of the present century, and a few are still in use.

In the eighties there was a great depression in the fishing business which impoverished the schooner fishermen to such an extent that many were forced to employ sloops in the Georges Bank fishery. The appearance of sloops on Georges, and the decline of the 'long-

A FRIENDSHIP SLOOP

shore fisheries, encouraged the Maine fishermen to employ sloops also. The sloop fishery out of Gloucester and its vicinity developed a type of sloop known as the "Essex sloop boats," one of a whole class of sloop-rigged vessels which may be classified as New England sloops. The Essex boats were powerful keel sloops, usually about 45 feet long.

These sloops having become familiar to the Maine fishermen, there was a natural tendency to replace the Muscongus Bay type with a deeper type, since shoal draft was no longer necessary.

The result was that a new type was developed, a reduced copy of the Essex, or Gloucester sloop in model. Due to limited means, the Maine sloop fishermen could not afford the larger boat. Since there was so close a connection between the Gloucester fleet and the Maine sloops, it is not surprising that the styles in Friendship sloops changed with those in the Essex sloops and schooners.

The Friendship sloops which went offshore worked winter and summer and so had to meet all kinds of weather. In summer they had to carry enough canvas to sail well in light airs, while in winter they had to face the necessity of beating home, heavily laden, against a howling winter nor'wester. This meant that the sloop had to be both stiff and weatherly, yet she had to have fine lines in order to sail fast, to compete for market with the rest of the fleet.

In the course of the development of this type, the Morse family, at Friendship, became the leading builders and designers. Their boats were widely copied in neighboring towns, but the sloops were always classed as "Friendship sloops" regardless of actual place of build.

Figure 9 hows a typical Friendship sloop of the offshore fishing class, modeled by Wilbur Morse about 1890. Boats of this class are among the most powerful of sailing craft, in comparison to their length, of any American types. An inspection of the sections in Figure 9 will show the reasons for this. Due to the shape of the mid-section, it was possible to locate the inside ballast very low in the hull, which, combined with the great beam, rather flat floors, hard bilges and wide, heavy quarters, enabled this sloop to stand up on her bottom and sail when an easier and sweeter-lined boat would be deck under. The comparatively long, straight run and flat quarters allow this type of hull to move very fast on a reach, or when running, and make for increased stability in windward work in hard going. Undoubtedly, sloops on this model were quite wet when punching into it, as they are rather wall-sided forward.

The rig has little to recommend it, as far as looks are concerned, but was typical of the period. The large area was necessary to drive the powerful hull in light weather, as the large amount of wetted surface and displacement, in proportion to length of hull, made resistance high at low speeds. Yet if this form of hull was not used, the vessel would not have power enough to work to windward in

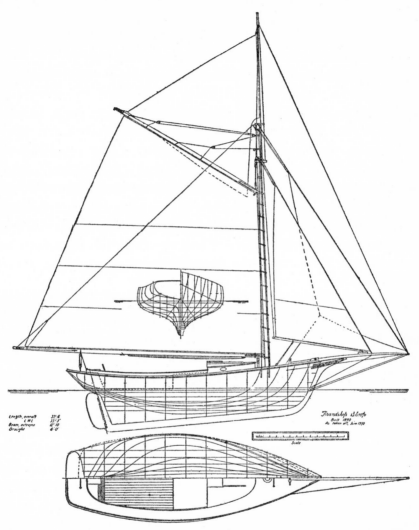

Figure 9. A Friendship sloop of 1890.
The topmast rig was typical of this period

heavy weather. It should be emphasized that great stability and weatherliness require a large area of sail to get the satisfactory combination. The recent attempts to combine heavy displacement and small sail area in one boat only prove that such a combination is impractical if even fair sailing qualities are expected. It is an unfortunate fact that heavy displacement, and its possibilities for increased accommodation, must be paid for by increased sail area, which, in turn, means greater labor in handling. The Friendship sloop illustrates this. If it had not been found necessary to have a large sail plan, the fishermen would not have paid the price to possess it.

Some of these sloops were fitted with live fish wells, and were therefore smacks, but most of them iced or salted their cargoes of fish. All had large non-self-bailing cockpits and a small cuddy forward. The ballast was gravel and small stones, as a rule. The rather long, high cutwater and trailboards are seen in all Friendship sloops, the name of the builder usually being carved or stamped into the trailboards. Another peculiarity at the bow is that there is rarely a gammoning iron on the bowsprit, which depends upon a few bolts and the bobstays for strength to withstand the pull of the headstays. The transom is always elliptical, as in the Essex schooners and sloops. This shape of stern and transom was introduced in Gloucester by the schooner *Ripple,* built at Essex in 1853 by Joseph Story. The tumble home of the quarters probably became popular because it prevented the fouling of the main sheet by hooking under the corner of a square transom. It is a very handsome stern, as well, and lightens the appearance of the heavy quarters. The length of the stern overhang gradually increased as the Friendship sloop developed.

Topmasts are no longer to be seen in the Friendship sloops, though the ironwork is sometimes noticeable on the older and larger boats. Some had spreaders and futtock shrouds, as in the drawing, but on most of them the topmast shrouds were brought down to the chain plates from over the spreaders. The long, low gaff was employed in the Gloucester schooners and sloops, as well as in these boats.

Few realize the close relationship of the Friendship sloop to the Gloucester schooner in both model and rig. When the improved schooners of the *Fredonia* model became popular at Gloucester the same hull features were used in reduced scale for an improved Friendship sloop. The model shown in Figure 9, however, remained a popular one and a large number of sloops were built from the same

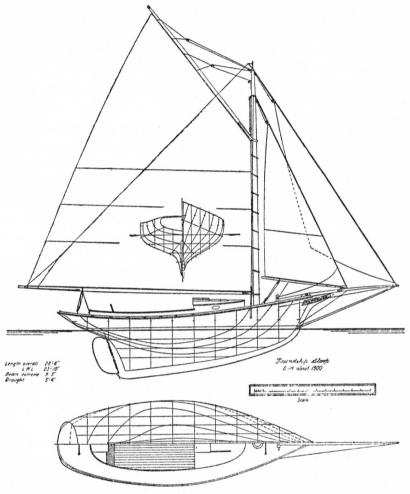

Length overall 28'6"
L.W.L 23'10"
Beam extreme 9'5"
Draught 5'4"

Friendship Sloop
Built about 1900

Scale

Figure 10. By 1900 the Friendship sloop had undergone considerable modification, both in line and rig, although retaining the general characteristics of the earlier model

lines, some variations being made, such as more or less sheer, the omitting of the swell of the rabbet, or decreased hollow of the garboards. Dimensions were also varied. The large offshore sloops were built well into the late nineties, but a decline in the offshore sloop fisheries decreased their number by 1900. Some of the large sloops found employment as cargo and farm boats, but most of them have disappeared. In winter the topmast was struck and left ashore; in summer, a topsail, and often a jib topsail, was also carried.

During the nineties a greatly improved sloop was introduced in the shore and lobster trade. The Friendship sloops, being no longer used in the offshore fisheries, became smaller. In the banks fishery a crew of three or more men wa carried, but in the shore fisheries two men, as a rule, comprised the crew. Hence the new boats omitted the cumbersome topsail and gear. Their hulls were made somewhat less powerful, and the improved model of the *Fredonia* was employed. This gave a more cutaway underbody profile and easier sections. The appearance of the rig was greatly improved by peaking up the gaff, but the comparative length of the spars remained the same. The power was much reduced by these improvements, but the ease of handling was greatly increased. The result was a sloop that was not only handsome, but handy, and sufficiently powerful to work to windward in anything but a hard gale, yet which was reasonably cheap to build.

Figure 10 shows a Friendship sloop of this improved type, which quickly became the most popular model among the shore fishermen. It is noticeable that the stern overhang is longer and the sheer more yacht-like, the lines being much easier than was the case in the earlier sloops. The draft was increased, in proportion to the over all length, but the displacement was proportionately reduced. This is the most suitable type for conversion to a yacht.

No particular rules appear to have been used in proportioning the hull, though the beam is usually one-third the over all length. The length of the spars seems to be of about the following proportions: length of mast equals length over all, plus half the depth; length of boom equals the over all length; length of gaff, such that when lowered its outer end comes to the transom; bowsprit, outboard, is equal to one-third the length of the boom. The mast is nearly perpendicular, and is placed about one-fifth of the l.w.l. length abaft the stem.

A study of these two plans will show how power to carry sail in heavy weather was procured. For considerations of cost, outside ballast could not be employed. Therefore, the inside ballast had to be located as low as possible, which was accomplished by hollow garboards, wide enough above the keel, however, to permit the larger proportion of the ballast to rest on top of the keel itself. Initial stability was further increased by the use of flat floors, beam and hard bilges, as has already been pointed out. Sharp lines were employed in order to get as much speed as was possible with the necessary displacement and sail area. However—and remember this—fine lines were not enough to make these sloops fast; they had to have a large rig, which meant more work to handle. The rig was certainly not one for weak men to handle in a blow. The offshore fishermen were strong, hardy men—they had to be to stand the hardships of the life. Imagine what it must have been like to beat home against a shrieking winter nor'wester in a small sloop. The deep reefs were put in the mainsail for a real purpose, not for the sake of appearance.

The reason for the cheapness of these sloops lies in their construction, which, it must be said, was poor. The workmanhip was fair, but the fastenings were slight, and the construction generally weak. Someone is going to ask why, if this is the case, the boats last as long as they do; the answer is that as long as they do not take the ground heavily their strength is not put to a severe test. Their construction will not stand much pounding, which is the only test of fastenings. There are some of these sloops now being used a yachts that are in a dangerous state and that need extensive repairs.

As an example of the construction, take this description of a 30-foot boat, with 10-foot beam. Her scantlings were as follows: keel, stem, sternpost and knees, oak; siding, about 4½ inches (there was no swell in the keel in this boat). Frames were of oak, steamed and bent, 1½" x 2¾" on the flat. It was noticeable that many frames were broken in the tuck, where the curvature is very hard. The frames are spaced 10 inches on centers, with no floors, the heels of the frames being nailed to the keel. There were few knees, two at the quarters and two at the partners, a block being worked in, in place of a breasthook. The fastenings were galvanized iron throughout. The deck was 2" x 2" pine, bent to the sweep of the sides. There were no clamps, shelves or stringers, their place being taken by the ¼-inch ceiling and a peculiar construction in the way of the planksheer. This consisted of a thick plank pieced together and fitted like an ordinary covering board, but instead of being on top of the deck beams it was at the underside of the deck planking, the heads of the frames being nailed to the outside of this plank and the deck beams notched into the inboard edge, flush on top. The deck planking was nailed to both the beams and to this plank wherever possible to strengthen the joining of the deck and sides. In this boat, the sheer plank appeared to be of oak, 2½ inches thick and about 8 inches wide in most places. The sheer plank ran from breasthook to transom knees. It will be seen that this construction takes the place of sheer clamp and shelf, its weakness being due more to improper fastenings than to poor design. The most serious weakness is the almost general lack of floors. The frames are alway bent on the flat, and are not as strong as desirable, allowing the hull to work a good deal as the age of the sloop increases. Taking out the ceiling is a risky procedure, as much of the stiffness of the hull is obtained from these members; yet the ceiling, usually carried too high, causes rot to set in.

It is apparent that the cheapness of the Friendship sloop, unlike that of the New Haven sharpie and the Chesapeake skipjack, was obtained through sacrifices in construction. These sloops cost little, a 28-footer cost only $780 in 1899. The same sloop built today, with good construction, would cost between $2,000 and $3,000. With the original type of construction she would cost between $1,500 and $2,000, the cost depending somewhat upon finish and accommodation. The model of the Friendship sloops is not a cheap one to build because of the hollow garboards and the shape of the stern; the swelling of the rabbet also increases the cost because of the labor required in molding it. Economy in this hull form can be had only by sacrificing finish and strength. Undoubtedly, another factor contributing to the low cost of these boats was the low cost of labor and materials at the time and place of their build.

THE FRIENDSHIP SLOOP

The Friendship sloop is quite popular with yachtsmen, and a large number of them have been converted to yachts by lengthening the cuddy, changing the rig and installing motors. They make very comfortable cruisers, but most of them are slow. This is due to the almost universal custom of cutting off the ends of both bowsprit and boom, thus reducing the sail area to a great extent and so spoiling the sailing qualities. This is done, of course, to make the rig

Construction Section

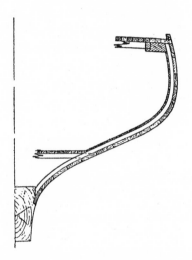

easier to handle. It would be infinitely better to put in a longer mast and to increase the hoist when the bowsprit and boom are cut down, so as to retain the same amount of sail area as the original rig. Due to the great stability of these sloops, they can carry the higher rig with safety.

Yacht designers, particularly in the region of Boston, have designed many modifications of the type. These are less powerful than the original type, and represent one of the best classes of any of the keel cruising sloops now popular. Such yacht adaptations usually have modern curved stems, as did some of the last of the Morse-built Friendship sloops. It is a pity that the beautiful clipper bow is not being retained in those built as yachts.

Friendship sloops have made long voyages. In 1931, a small

sloop of this type was stolen at Quincy, Mass., and the "pirate" appears to have sailed her to the coast of Holland single-handed — at least her wreckage was found there. The man who took her lost her and his life through the lack of heavy ground tackle. Another small sloop was reported to be on her way across the Atlantic in June, 1932.

These sloops are eminently suitable for deep-water cruising and racing; they are undoubtedly superior to some of the much-touted foreign types that have received so much attention of late.

Chapter Four

⚓

THE CAPE COD CATBOAT

Chapter Four

⚓

THE CAPE COD CATBOAT

THE history of the American catboat previous to 1850 is a matter of conjecture, even the source of the name being shrouded in mystery. It is commonly believed that the cat is a descendant of some early Dutch type, but it is far more likely that the cat is a modification of the old centerboard sloops of the 40's, so common in New York waters in those days. These sloops were designed to work under mainsail alone, when desirable, so it was natural that a type should evolve that would require no headsail. Undoubtedly, the cat rig was a much older institution than the catboat, and may have developed from an early Dutch rig, but it must be remembered that the cat rig was used in other types long before the catboat, as such, was known. At any rate, in hull form, there was a close similarity between the cat and the centerboard sloop. The early sloops often had a cat rig in addition to the regular rig, and could race as either sloops or cats. The old sandbaggers were an example of this. From this, it is apparent that the two types must have been closely related.

That the catboat originated in the vicinity of New York is highly probable, and by 1850 the type was quite common there. The most famous of catboat builders of the period was Bob Fish. The influence of this man was marked, and two of his boats introduced the type abroad. In 1852, one of his cats was taken to England where her qualities astonished yachtsmen. This boat was called the *Una,* and thereafter cats were called "una-boats" in England. Later, another was sold to Germany, and there received the name "bobfish." The plans of the *Una* appeared in Dixon Kemp's *Man-*

ual of Yacht and Boat Sailing. The early New York cats were small, low-sided boats, suitable for smooth water sailing only. They had a low, peaked sail, short gaff, long boom, and a rather great hoist. Judging by the drawings and half-models now in existence, they were apparently boats of slight sheer.

During the 50's the type spread to neighboring waters, particularly those of New Jersey and Connecticut, and by the end of the decade the cat was popular as far east as Rhode Island. Due to the more exposed waters in which they were used, the eastern cats were more able boats. Newport and Bristol, in Rhode Island, became building centers for this class. The Rhode Island cat was a well-formed boat, having moderate sheer, a straight keel and rabbet, with stem and transom nearly perpendicular to the bottom of the keel. They also had a good deal of deadrise, though there were some cats built on the sharpie model. The early Rhode Island cats appear to have been employed wholly as commercial craft, and were usually referred to as "Newport cats."

Until the late 60's a type of small sloop, usually a centerboarder, was employed by the fishermen of Cape Cod. In 1860 an Osterville boatbuilder, Horace S. Crosby, built the first cat on the Cape. Mr. Crosby had undoubtedly seen the Rhode Island cats, and had admired them. He seems, however, to have had ideas for improving the type. At any rate, his boat was so successful that copies soon replaced the earlier sloops. The type developed very quickly, and by 1870 the Cape cats were considered a separate type. The conditions along the Cape shore were far more trying than those with which other classes of cats had to contend. The Cape has always been regarded as a dangerous place for small craft. Most of the fishing was done out of towns on the south shore, Chatham, Hyannis, Osterville, and Falmouth. The Chatham fishery, in particular, was of large proportions. Chatham men worked off Pollock Rip, often going thirty miles or more offshore. Fully exposed to the sweep of the Atlantic, and with only shoal harbors for shelter, the Chatham boats had to be seaworthy and weatherly. The shoals are very extensive in this vicinity, and the tides are strong. It will be seen that the requirements of the fishermen in this section were quite difficult to meet. Furthermore, the crews of the boats consisted of not more than two men, and the boats were raced to market. In other words, shoal draft, speed, seaworthiness, weatherliness, handiness, and cheapness were the necessary features of design. As the boats usually came home each night, the cabin accommodations were small.

A CAPE COD CATBOAT

Most yachtsmen think of the cat as merely a smooth water boat, but it is evident that the fishermen did not consider it so. Like any shoal draft boat with a large cockpit, the cat required intelligent handling. That the cats were safe craft, ordinarily, is borne out by the fact that the loss of life, due to foundering, was not great along the Cape shore. Much has been written of the faults of the cats, their dangerous behavior when running before a heavy wind and sea, their reputed tendency to capsize, the difficulty in reefing, due to the overhang of the boom beyond the transom, and

49

their tendency toward hard steering, particularly when reefed down.

While these objections may well apply to many cats, they do not apply to all. The chief difficulty with the catboat has been the over-development which has resulted in an attempt to procure speed. Many cats, built as yachts, carried far too much sail, and such boats were bound to have objectionable features. Inexperienced handling, combined with too much sail, was undoubtedly the cause of the loss of life at summer resorts, which has been one of the reasons for the prejudice against catboats among modern yachtsmen. Some years ago, after the big racing cats had come in favor, many yachting writers attacked the cat type, accusing it of all possible bad qualities, which could be illustrated by reference to that over-developed class. These writers were attempting to create support for deep keel craft, adherents of which most of them seem to have been. In spite of the claims of these men, it is possible to find cats that do not exhibit the bad qualities mentioned, which seems to indicate that the faults are not inherent in the cat, but rather, are the result of poor design in individual boats.

It must be admitted that the cat rig and hull are not desirable in boats exceeding 28 feet over all. This limitation makes full headroom out of the question, but such dimensions make full headroom impracticable in any type. Having listed the objections to the cat, it is only fair that the advantages should receive equal attention. The cats are relatively cheap to build and maintain, if the original form is adhered to; they are easy to get underway, due to the simplicity of the rig; there is a surprising amount of room in the cabin because of the great amount of beam for the length; the draft is small; they are usually fast and weatherly; they can be rigged so as to be handy and to be reasonably seaworthy for their size; they can be fitted to make rather good single-handers; and last but not least, they make good auxiliaries, as the hull form is such that it can be driven (at speeds not in excess of ten miles per hour), with small power, which means low first cost and operating expense in the power plant.

It has been said that the cat should be a "box," but this is not

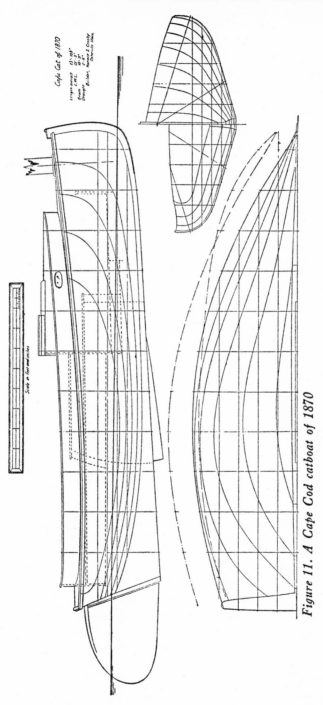

Figure 11. A Cape Cod catboat of 1870

true. It will be shown that the Cape cats, at least, were well formed, and it will be seen that their lines are symmetrical.

Beginning in 1870 — to show the development of the type under discussion — Figure 11 was a cat built by Horace S. Crosby during that year. She is not as handsome as later cats, but her lines are good. The lack of sheer spoils her appearance, yet she was undoubtedly a good sailer. With her slack bilges and rising floor, her stability was moderate. She would be rather fast under reefed sail; in fact, this hull required little sail to drive it. Attention is called to the raking midsection so necessary in a beamy hull; this permits a longer run than would otherwise be possible. It will be noted that there is a marked hollow in the entrance, but there is no "shoulder" in the water lines. Some builders claim that the hollow increases weatherliness by creating a "lee surge" at the bow. The run is very well formed for speed; the buttocks show a good clearance. 24 to 26 feet over all is the standard size of these working cats.

The cats of this period steered with tillers, but by 1880 wheels replaced the tillers. It is likely that many of the old cats were badly balanced and were brutes to steer with tillers. Up until the 70's, the corners of the cockpit and cabin trunk were angular, but this feature was replaced by the steam-bent coamings seen in modern cats. The centerboard was farther aft at this time than at a later date, as the lower peak of the gaff caused the center of effort to be well aft. This necessitated placing the greatest beam and the centers of lateral plane and buoyancy well aft, as well. Many of the Cape cats had their centerboards off center, dropping alongside the keel rather than through it. This was considered the strongest construction. The sail plan is shown in Figure 15. The spar lengths were noted on the half-model from which these lines were taken; details are from contemporary plans and photos.

Figure 12 shows the next step in the development of the Cape cats. This boat was built by the Crosbys in 1883, for Chatham owners. She was a handsomer boat than the earlier example, having a more graceful sheer. Her lines differ but little from Figure 11, except that power is even more reduced by more rise to the floors, and lighter quarters. Cats built on these lines were in great favor, as

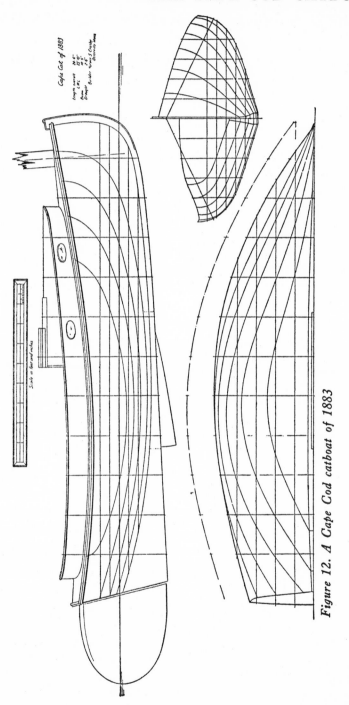

Figure 12. A Cape Cod catboat of 1883

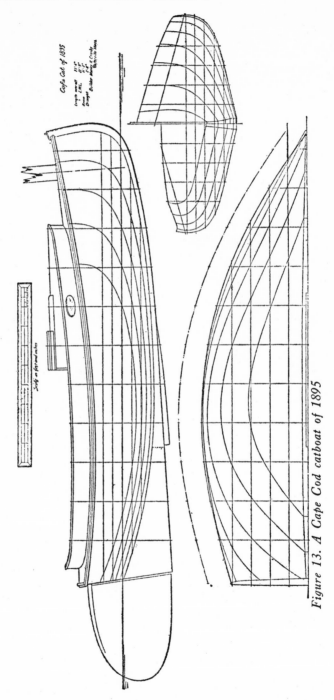

Figure 13. A Cape Cod catboat of 1895

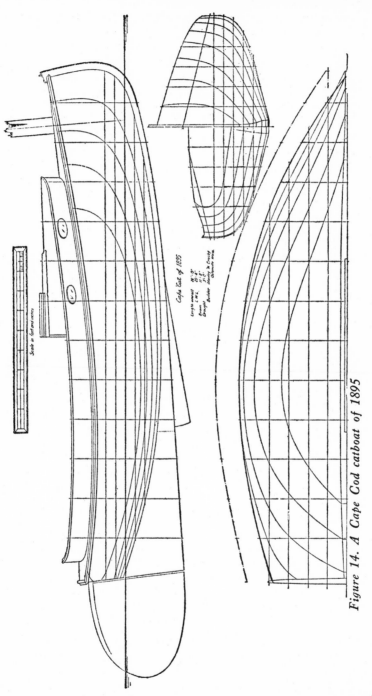

Cape Cat of 1895

Length overall   18'-0"
Beam L.W.L.   15'-4"
Beam   8'-2"
Draught   1'-5"
Builder   Manley H. Crosby
            Osterville Mass.

Scale in feet and meters

Figure 14. A Cape Cod catboat of 1895

they required only a relatively small sail area to drive them, and hence were easier to handle. This represents a seaworthy type, as long as the boat is not over-canvased.

The good qualities of these cats of moderate power were responsible for the popularity of the catboat in later years. During the 70's and 80's a great many yachts were built on the Cape cat model. These usually had short counters, the transom being set at a great rake, as a rule. Some boats were built with the transom almost vertical, however. All these boats had inboard rudderposts and the rudders were practically wholly submerged. The counter was thought, by some, to improve the appearance of the cat, but experienced catboat sailors claim that the flat transom and "barn-door" rudder made for a faster boat. Most of the counter-sterned cats submerged a little of their transom when in sailing trim, so no sailing·length was gained, and rudder area was usually lost.

During the remaining years of the nineteenth century the "improvement" of the cat went on; long overhangs were tried, hollow floors and reverse curves in the run were used, and a large sail area became the fashion. Large classes of racing cats appeared, the Quincy Class on Massachusetts Bay being the best known. Such fast cats as *Harbinger, Scat, Varuna, Step Lively, Magic, Lazy Jack, Almira,* and other cracks, appeared. Fast though these boats were, their sail area was far too great for either safety or ease of handling. The Crosbys, Bacon, Hanley, and Babbit, were well known builders of racers. The increasing cost and dangerous rig of the racing cat caused the decline of the class, and the only fleet of racing cats now active is on Barnegat Bay, in New Jersey.

As the years went by, the cats became more and more powerful, their initial stability increasing as the sail area became larger. Not only did this change take place in cat yachts, but also in working cats. Figure 13 illustrates the increase of initial stability that had taken place by 1895. This cat was built by Manley H. Crosby as a fishing boat. Though she is somewhat shorter than the earlier examples, her beam is actually greater, and, with her harder bilges, she could carry about as much sail as the larger boats. The hollow in the entrance is not so marked as in the earlier cats, the bow being

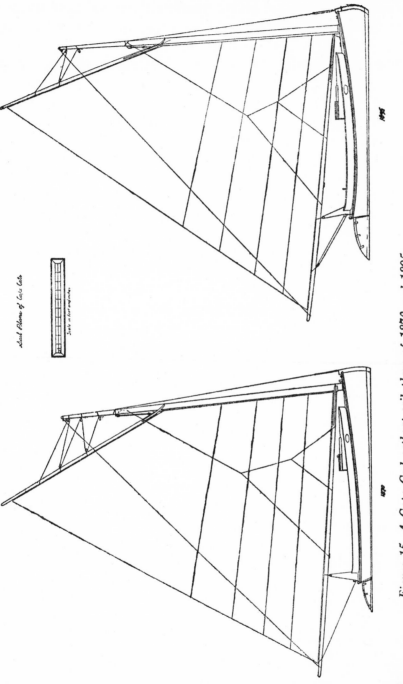

Keel Plans of Cats Cats

Scale in feet and inches

Figure 15. A Cape Cod catboat sail plans of 1870 and 1895

57

more cut away at the forefoot. The run is very well formed, and the buttock lines are pleasing. On the whole, this is a handsome and seaworthy cat.

Figure 14 is another cat of the same year and by the same builder. This boat is not only larger than Figure 13, but is also more powerful. The manner in which this increase of initial stability is obtained is interesting. By studying the run of this boat, it will be seen that the quarters are quite heavy and that the deadrise at the transom is somewhat less than amidships. This is the same type of run as that seen in modern displacement power boats, which accounts for the good behavior of the cat under power. The lines of this cat are very good, from the standpoint of speed, but she would require a large spread of canvas to obtain the desired results.

Figures 13 and 14 may be taken as examples of modern Cape Cod cats, as there has been practically no change in hull form since their time. The addition of a motor made no difference in their form, as the deadwood needed only to be cut for the propeller aperture. The motor is usually located under a box in the cockpit.

Figure 15 illustrates the changes in rig that took place between 1870 and 1895. It will be seen that the chief change was in the peak of the gaff, which increased as the type developed. In late years the sail has almost taken the shape of the sliding gunter. The early cat was cheaply rigged; there were no special fittings. There were no shrouds and only one stay which set up to the stemhead with a lanyard. The cat sailors claim that a cat does better with this stay slack rather than when set up taut. For this reason some of the small cats omitted the forestay altogether. The running rigging consisted of the throat and peak halliards, the main sheet, topping lift, and, in some boats, the lazy jacks. The main sheet had few parts; most boats had to be luffed before the sheet could be flattened. The topping lift was an important piece of gear. It rove through a block at the masthead and a fairlead block on deck, the fall belaying to a cleat on the cockpit coaming within reach of the helmsman. Due to the overhang of the boom beyond the transom, a reefing tackle of some sort was necessary. This was usually a pennant with a hook spliced into one end, which was hooked into the reef cringle, the fall reeving through a cheek-block and belaying on a cleat on the boom. This was a heavy line as it was often under great strain; in rough water it was sometimes impossible to pass the outer reef points, so the pennant had to act as an outhaul. Since the boom overhung the transom as much as 12 feet in a 26-foot cat, it was often necessary to stand on the sheet to reef. On some boats the end of the boom could be reached by standing on the rudder. It was the custom to reef some racing cats from the tender.

Some of the working cats had plank bowsprits which were short and served only to give spread to the forestay and as a cathead, no sail being set on the forestay. Some racing cats set a jib on a similar spar, more to cheat a rule than because they needed it. A few of these racing cats were out of balance and, in such cases, the jib made steering easier. There should be no necessity for setting a jib in a well-designed cat. None of the working cats had a spreader on the forestay, but some racing cats did because of the strain brought on the masthead by the very long gaffs and booms. Some of these big cats required shrouds, set up to outriggers over each bow.

The size of the catboat varies from 11 to 32 feet on the load water line, the beam varying from 5 to 14 feet. During the 80's and 90's, large cats, about 30 to 32 feet long on the water line, 13 to 14 feet beam, and 3 or 3½ feet draft, were built at Osterville for party boats for use at Nantucket and other resorts. These were used only in good weather. With fishermen, the most popular size of cat is between 22 and 26 feet over all length. The Chatham boats were 24 to 26 feet in length.

The catboat is a national type and should be more popular among yachtsmen, as it is suitable for the type of sailing most of us do. For knocking around in sheltered waters and alongshore, for day sailing and week-end cruising, the cat is a splendid type. In fact, the Cape cat is suitable for any type of cruising, except offshore. The boats just described merit greater favor from yachtsmen than they have received in late years.

Chapter Five

⚓

THE GLOUCESTER SCHOONER: I

Chapter Five

⚓

THE GLOUCESTER SCHOONER: I

THE Gloucester fishing schooners need no introduction to yachtsmen. Fast, seaworthy and handsome, they have long been admired by all seamen. The early types are of particular interest as
they influenced the design of many other classes of schooners in
America.

The development of the fast sailing Gloucester schooner may be
said to have started with the building of the little *Romp*. The advantages of speed in a fishing schooner were first appreciated by the
Essex modeler and builder, Andrew Story, who, in order to demon-
strate these advantages to the conservative fishermen, built a small
schooner on speculation during the winter of 1846-47. This vessel
was the famous *Romp*. Taking the then well-known Baltimore clipper schooner as a model, Andrew Story turned out a vessel that retained most of the speed of the fast southern schooners, but with
added capacity, seaworthiness and dryness. The new schooner had
the low freeboard, deep drag to the keel, raking ends, straight sheer,
and marked deadrise of the Baltimore flyers, combined with harder
bilges and longer body, to give cargo capacity. Her bow, too, differed from that of a typical Baltimore schooner in that it was very
round and full on deck, but due to the great flare employed was
rather sharp on the water line.

So wedded to the old types were the fishermen that it was some
time before Story could sell his vessel. At last a man who had lost
his old vessel was prevailed upon to purchase the new schooner.
When it came time to fit out, great difficulty was found in getting
men to sail on her, as she was considered too sharp for safety. At

63

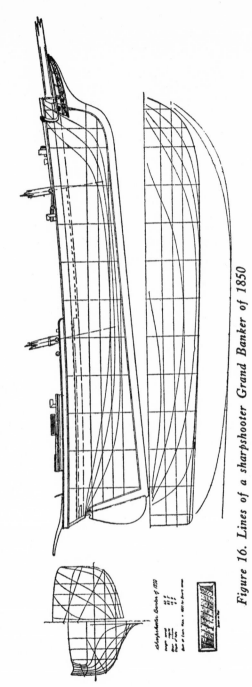

Figure 16. Lines of a sharpshooter Grand Banker of 1850

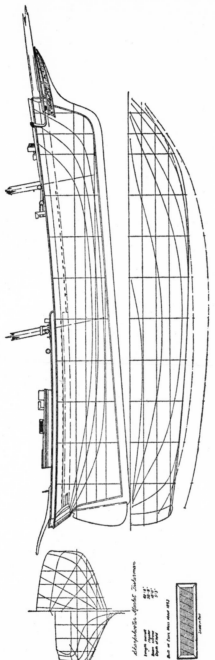

Figure 17. A sharpshooter market fisherman built in 1853

last a crew was procured and the *Romp* got to sea, not without many misgivings on the part of the waterfront "experts." By the time the *Romp* had reached the fishing banks her reputation was established; not only had she proved her seaworthiness and speed to her own doubting crew, but to those of all vessels she had met.

Her success established by her first trip, copies of the new schooner were at once built. Because of the great deadrise usually employed, vessels of the new type were soon nicknamed "file-bottoms," and, later, "sharpshooters." After a short career as a fisherman, the *Romp* carried a party of gold-seekers around Cape Horn to California. Fom 1849 to 1857, the sharpshooter was the popular type of fisherman, but during the late 50's the model underwent a rapid change.

From builders' half-models, sailmakers' plans, pictures, and a few rigged models that are contemporary, it is possible to show just what the sharpshooter looked like. In Figure 16 will be seen the lines of a sharpshooter banker built at Essex in 1850, for Beverly owners. The bankers, because they stayed out on the banks until they had a full cargo of fish, or "fare" salted down, were more of the carrier type than were the market boats which made rapid trips to the inshore banks and brought home fresh fish in wet wells, or iced. The banker in Figure 16, it will be noticed, was quite burdensome for her length. The full, round, and sharply flaring bow shown was known at Essex as the "cartwheel bow," and was considered necessary to prevent the vessel from diving when at anchor on the banks in heavy weather.

To illustrate the difference between the banker and the market boat, the lines of a sharpshooter market schooner are shown in Figure 17. This vessel was built at Essex about 1853, and is, for her time, an extremely sharp schooner. It will be noticed that her displacement is relatively less than that of the banker, and that she is much sharper. The necessity of speed was greater in the case of the market boats than in that of the bankers, as fresh fish do not long remain in good condition.

The heads of the sharpshooters were long and had a pointed look; the bowsprit had little steeve, often being "hogged" down, as in the Chesapeake skipjacks or bugeyes of more recent times. The heads were supported by a single headrail on each side, and by cheek knees and carved trail boards, finishing off forward with a simple billet or fiddle-head. The sterns had very little overhang. The early sharpshooters had the old-fashioned transom, the lower portion of which was set at a more acute angle than the upper, and the rudder stock went up through the lower transom face rather than

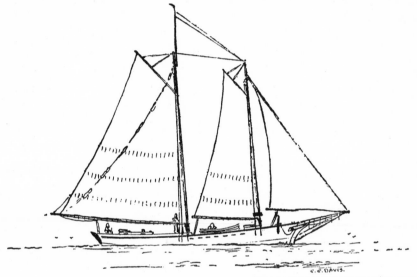

AN EARLY TYPE GLOUCESTERMAN

through the counter, as was almost universally the case after 1850. The top of the transom was square-cornered, but as the mainsheet had a tendency to catch these corners, the elliptical transom seen on modern schooners was introduced in the beautiful little sharpshooter *Ripple,* built at Essex in 1853 by Joseph Story. One of the first schooners to have the long overhang counter was the *Break O' Day,* put up in 1859, but a number of years passed before this type of stern became general in the fishing fleet.

The sharpshooters were built of oak throughout, except for the decks, which were of white pine. The planking was between two and three inches thick up to the level of the quarter deck plank-

67

sheer, and a three-inch band of white was painted along this plank-sheer and carried forward to the stem. Above, there were a couple of strakes of thin planking, an inch or so in thickness, extending to the rail cap. The line formed by the two thicknesses of planking is the waist, and up to the late 60's, the waist in the sharpshooters was

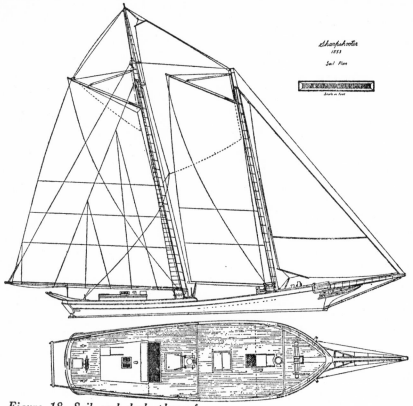

Figure 18. Sail and deck plan of sharpshooter shown in Figure 17

at the quarter deck planksheer level. Later it was a few inches above the quarter deck scuppers. The topsides were painted black or dark green, the underbody green or copper color and the decks and fittings gray or white. Sometimes there was a multi-colored stripe above the planksheer and below the "waist."

Figure 18 represents the sail and deck plans of the schooner shown in Figure 17. The rig was simple, differing but little from the then popular pilot boat rig. The masts had a strong rake and there was a bonnet in the jib. The only difference between the rig of the bankers and that shown was that the former was relatively smaller and a maintopsail was rarely carried, though sometimes a dummy maintopmast was rigged. The deck plan was almost standardized until comparatively recent years. Beginning forward, there was a pump brake windlass (the handspike windlass was used in the 40's), abaft this was the wooden jib sheet horse extending from bulwark to bulwark, supported by bulwark stanchions, which also supported cavil cleats. This horse was five or six inches in diameter, square at the ends, and some five inches above the deck. At each end, about eighteen inches inboard of the bulwarks, a bolt was driven, with its head flush, and extending about three inches below the horse. These bolts acted as stops for the traveler, which was a plain iron ring. Then came the foremast, with either a wooden collar for belaying pins, or a fife rail. The forecastle companionway was close abaft the foremast, and was combined with a small hatch to the hold. The two openings had a common coaming, about 4'-8" long and 36 inches wide, and were separated by a beam under which was a bulkhead. The forward of the two openings was covered by a slide and companionway, which overhung the coaming forward almost to the mast. This was the entrance to the forecastle. The after opening was covered by an ordinary hatch cover and a portable grating. Amidships was the main hatch, about 4'-6" square, and abaft this the "great beam," or break in the deck, the rise to the quarter deck being from eight to ten inches.

On the quarter deck was the foresheet horse, of iron, and the mainmast, with its fife rail, came next. Just abaft the mainmast and under the fife rail were two wooden pumps, bored out of solid logs, eight or nine inches in outside diameter, extending up about 26 inches, to the underside of the fife rails, through which holes were bored to enable the pump plungers to be lifted out. The plungers were operated by levers pivoted on iron brackets shaped somewhat like oarlocks, the shanks of which extended through the fife rail and also the deck.

Abaft the pumps was another hatch, 4 feet long and 4'-6" wide. Then came a large grating laid on deck just forward of the cabin trunk. Sometimes a deck box replaced the after portion of the grating. The cabin trunk had no ports. There was a slide and a skylight on the roof, and also the stack of the cabin stove. Many schooners had a long "barrel head box" on the fore end of the trunk. Abaft the trunk was the wheelbox (tillers were used in the 40's), and the quarter bitts. The main sheet horse, of iron, was on the "seat" over the transom, but sometimes quarter blocks were used. Wooden stern davits were used to carry a boat.

From 1855 to 1860 there was a period of experimentation, the desire for speed in the fishing schooners having become almost a mania. However, there were some conservative models still built. Figure 19 shows one of these, a banker. On these lines, the *Lookout* was built, in 1857, at Essex. Designed by Charles O. Story and built in the yard of Joseph Story, the *Lookout* was a popular vessel for use on the Grand Banks and the Georges. So well was she liked that some twenty other schooners were built on her moulds during the next ten years. Though a good carrier, the *Lookout* was much sharper than the banker of the 50's. Even in this class of vessel there was a marked decrease in depth.

It was in the market fleet that the more extreme schooners were developed. During the late 50's, each new market schooner was shoaler, wider, and sharper-ended than the last, until the new "clippers" came into existence about 1857. Heralded by two extreme schooners modeled by Charles O. Story, the *Etta G. Fogg* and the *George Fogg, built* at Essex in that year, the clippers soon replaced the older type. The two mentioned were built for Wellfleet owners and were employed in the market fishery in the summer and in the Chesapeake Bay oyster trade during the winter. They were shoal, keel vessels, in order to enter the southern oyster ports, and were very fast. The success of these and similar schooners soon led to vessels of even more extreme type.

Such a schooner is shown in Figure 20, the *Flying Fish,* modeled and built by Jeremiah Burnham in 1860 at Essex, as a fast market schooner. Though considered an extreme vessel when built,

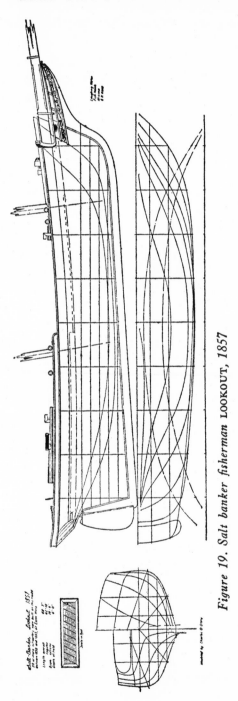

Figure 19. Salt banker fisherman LOOKOUT, *1857*

she was a common type for the next 25 years. The *Flying Fish* was an extremely fast ship; in fact, for some years she was looked upon as being the fastest schooner in the fleet. After being employed as a fisherman for some time, she was sold to New London for use as a sealer and sea elephant hunter, though it would seem difficult to find a type more unsuited to the rigors of the weather off Cape Stiff than this high-hatted, Essex-built flyer.

The lines of the *Flying Fish* show the characteristics of the clipper type. Perhaps the most apparent of these were the shoalness of the hull and its very marked hollowness at bow and stern. Compared to the older sharpshooters, the clipper had little drag and lower bilges, combined with great proportionate beam. Practically all of this type had very raking midsections, remarkably long hollow runs, and, usually, rather heavy quarters. From all accounts, the clippers sailed best when nearly on even keel, probably because of the heavy lee quarter which was a drag when well heeled. When rolled down, rails under, they were apt to capsize or to take a knockdown.

In appearance, the clipper was distinguished by her low freeboard, rather short counter, and the typical long, heavy head. Many of the heads seen on vessels of this class had one more headrail than is shown in the plan of the *Flying Fish*. This rail was above the long rail (to the underside of the cathead), was supported by iron rods to the rail below, and reached from the billet to the foreside of the catheads. Only the large vessels seem to have had this feature.

These vessels were painted very like the sharpshooters, and had the same white band along the quarter deck planksheer and forward; when the waist line was raised (some time in the late 60's, apparently), another stripe was added, of red, just above the quarter deck scuppers. Some time in the 70's, the practice of painting the bulwarks a dark bottle green, with the remaining portion of the hull black, became popular, and finally, it became fairly common to see hulls all green, the shade being either an olive or dark bottle green. Red copper paint became very popular in the Gloucester fleet soon after the Civil War.

As employed on the fishing schooner, the catheads were small,

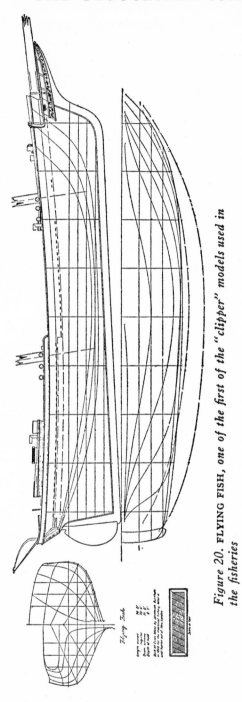

Figure 20. FLYING FISH, one of the first of the "clipper" models used in the fisheries

with but little spread. They were merely bolted to the bulwark stanchions after the planking had been put on. The long headsail widened as it approached and curved up to the underside of the cathead.

Figure 21 shows the deck and sail plan of the *Flying Fish,* the

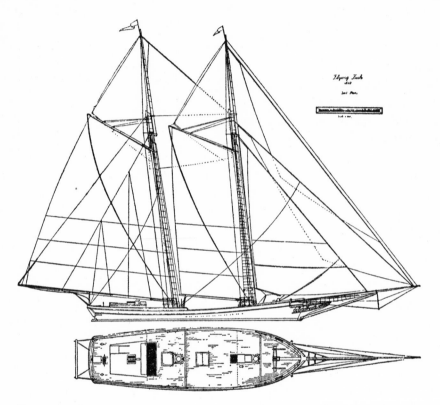

Figure 21. Deck and sail plan of FLYING FISH, *1860*

last being taken from the sailmaker's drawings. The deck arrangement varies but little from that seen in the sharpshooters, and requires no further comment. The height of some of the deck structures was as follows: samson post, 4 feet; windlass bitts, 3'-6"; fife rails, 28 to 30 inches; companionway, 2'-3" at after end, 20 inches at the fore, exclusive of a slide 3 inches high. The hatch coamings were from 12 to 14 inches high; the topsail bitts supporting the fore end of the main fife rail, 42 inches, or thereabouts. The cabin trunk was usually quite high in the clippers, varying from 30 to 36 inches in height above the quarter deck; the quarter bitts were 21 inches in height and sided about 8 inches.

The rig is worthy of attention, if for no other reason than its size. While the contemporary bankers, such as *Lookout,* carried a small edition of the same sail plan, they rarely had foretopmasts. The market schooners, however, had a complete rig, as shown. Only in winter were the topmasts and jibboom left at home. All standing rigging was of hemp, as in the sharpshooters, the jibstay being about three inches in diameter. The jibstay passed through the bowsprit and shackled into the stem, while the bobstay reached from the stem to a band on the bowsprit. Both were tarred and wrapped with canvas, with a rawhide cover, to a few feet above the water line. Chain was sometimes used for the lower bobstay. The jib hanks were of wood, as were the mast ings. The big jib had a bonnet, and this practice was carried well into the 80's. In old photographs the jibboom is usually shown well "hogged" down. Because of the long boom and the position of the main sheet, breakage was very common and it was the custom to take along a number of timbers to "fish" the spar when an accident occurred. The jibboom was usually on the side of the bowsprit, to clear the jibstay.

In spite of the danger incurred in the use of this type, the clippers were widely copied because of their speed. It is also claimed, by old men who sailed in them, that when hove-to they were more comfortable than the more able modern schooners, having a tendency to slide to leeward on the face of a comber. At any rate, the coasters, West Indian fruiters, and the fishermen built in Maine and Nova Scotia, were copies of the Essex-built clippers. It took many years and great loss of lives and vessels to convince fishermen that a better type was possible.

Chapter Six

⚓

THE GLOUCESTER SCHOONER: II

THE GLOUCESTER SCHOONER: II

THE trend of the design of Gloucester fishing schooners during the period between 1870 and the early 1880's was toward such extremes of the so-called "clipper" type as were apparent in the *Grace L. Fears,* Figure 22. This vessel had all the characteristics of her type — low, hard bilges, low bulwarks, shallow hold and a large rig. She was built at Gloucester by David Alfred Story in 1874. On the same molds other schooners were built during the next few years, among them the *Bunker Hill.* The *Fears* is best remembered as the schooner from which Howard Blackburn became separated, bringing about the death of his dory-mate and his long row to shore, the result of which was the loss of his hands and toes from freezing. Such vessels as the *Fears* were popular in all classes of the fisheries, even on the Grand Banks, during these years.

During the eighties, Captain J. W. Collins, a Gloucester skipper, joined the United States Fish Commission and, conscious that much of the fearful loss of lives and vessels could be traced to the bad features of the type of schooner then in use, began to write on the necessity of a new class of vessel. The Gloucester newspapers carried this discussion in their columns and much argument resulted. The builders and modelers gave thought to the subject and, in 1884, the famous *Roulette* was launched at East Boston, by Dennison J. Lawlor. Lawlor was born in New Brunswick and started modeling and building at East Boston about 1850. Though he had built a number of fishing schooners, such as the *Sylph* in '65 the *Sarah H. Cressy* in '66 and the *Helen M. Foster* in '71, he was best known as the designer and builder of pilot boats. In the same

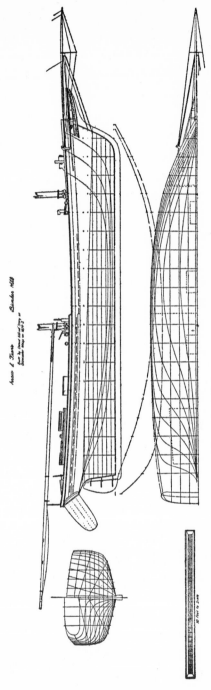

Figure 22. GRACE L. FEARS, built in 1874, is typical of the trend in design between 1870 and 1880

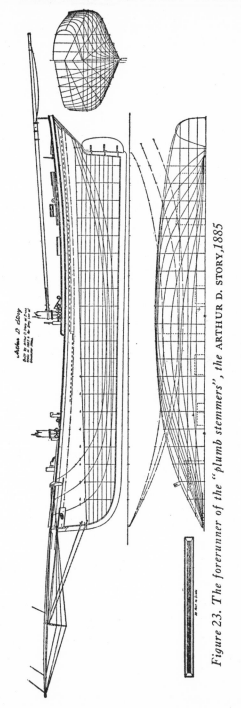

Figure 23. The forerunner of the "plumb stemmers", the ARTHUR D. STORY, 1885

year that he laid down the *Roulette,* he built the great *Hesper,* long considered the fastest of all pilot schooners.

The *Roulette* was a sensation. Not only was she about two feet deeper in the hold and much sharper in the floors than any of her contemporaries, but she proved to be a very fast sailer and more weatherly than any schooner in the fleet. Though the *Roulette* was built for a Philadelphia firm, she usually worked out of Boston, and during the latter part of her existence was owned there.

While the *Roulette* was building at East Boston, the other builders and designers were not idle. Captain Collins had been on friendly terms with Lawlor and with his help had modeled a new schooner for the Fish Commission, which was laid down at Noank, Conn., and launched the next year (1885). At about the same time, Arthur D. Story began to build a schooner on pilot boat lines at Essex. The *Roulette* had a plumb stem but also had a gammon knee head, which did not improve her appearance. The pilot schooners had been given plumb and straight stems for many years, and the two new schooners followed this style. The Fish Commission's new schooner was named the *Grampus* and was quite successful. The Essex vessel, Figure 23, was launched about the same time as the *Grampus* and was named for her builder, *Arthur D. Story*. She was employed mostly as a banker, going to Iceland regularly for cod. Eventually she was lost with all hands. It is said that she and another schooner were driven under, side by side, while under a press of sail.

The plan of the *Arthur D. Story* may be taken as an example of the new class of fishing schooner. Unfortunately, I am unable to find out who modeled her; perhaps Lawlor should have credit for her, too. The new pilot boat model fishing schooners had the same rig as the older boats; the change was in lines and size. It may be interesting to compare the vessels already mentioned. The *Fears* measured 84.50 tons net, 81 feet long, 22.9 feet beam and 8.4 feet depth of hold; the *Roulette* was 79.15 tons net, 82 feet long, 23.2 feet beam, and 10 feet depth of hold; the *Grampus* was 83.3 tons net, 81 feet long, 22.4 feet beam, and 10 feet depth of hold, and the *Story* was 98.61 tons net, 85 feet long, 23.3 feet beam, and 9.6 feet depth of hold. These measurements, it should be noted, are for tonnage and

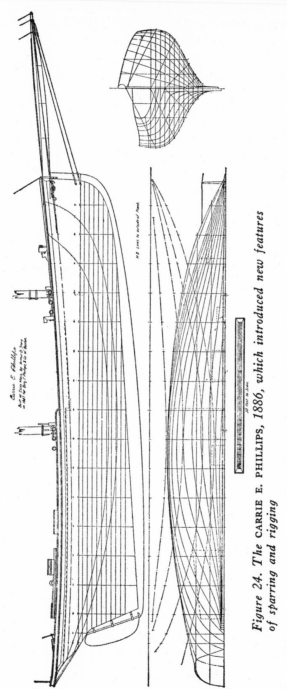

Figure 24. The CARRIE E. PHILLIPS, *1886, which introduced new features of sparring and rigging*

are not strictly accurate; however, they give a measure of comparison. It will be seen that there was a great increase in carrying capacity in the new vessels in addition to a change of form. The pilot schooner model introduced a new type of stern, as will be seen in the plans of the *Story,* which was popular for a few years. The success of the vessels built in 1884 and 1885 resulted in a number of "plumb stemmers," such as the *Puritan,* in 1887, and the *J. H. Carey,* in 1888, all fine, able schooners. However, a new vessel that was to mark the turning point in the Gloucester fleet had come out about this time.

In 1886, Benjamin Phillips, of Boston, commissioned the rising young yacht designer, Edward Burgess, to draw plans for a fast, big schooner, and Arthur D. Story built her at Essex that winter. This was the well-known *Carrie E. Phillips,* Figure 24. She measured 109.99 tons net, was 93.5 feet long, 24.9 feet beam, and 11 feet depth of hold. The *Phillips* was an innovation in more ways than one and she was even deeper and with more rising floors than the earlier schooners; she had a more rockered keel than had yet been tried in a fisherman; she introduced many new features of masting and rigging, such as the spike bowsprit with a spreader through the stem, a short foremast and improved ironwork. She was one of the first, if not the first, fisherman to have wire standing rigging. There were changes on deck and below as well; the old double hatch forward was dropped, and so were the wooden catheads. Below, the forecastle was lengthened to give greater accommodation. The *Phillips,* in spite of her increased dimensions, was considered a small carrier; she lasted 12 years, "going lost" in August, 1899. This schooner had a big reputation for speed and was noted for her looks.

Among the major changes brought about by the advent of the *Phillips* was the bringing of the headstay to the gammoning iron, resulting in the disappearance of the big jib and the introduction of the modern double-headsail rig. She was, incidentally, one of very few fishing schooners out of New England ports that was painted white, in the yacht fashion, but, naturally, this did not prove very satisfactory.

Though the *Phillips* introduced many of the features seen in fishermen today, it must not be supposed that all schooners built immediately after her were fitted in the same manner. For some years, a number of schooners were built with jibbooms, while those with spike bowsprits often had the forestay a few feet forward of the gammoning iron, and a fairly big jib.

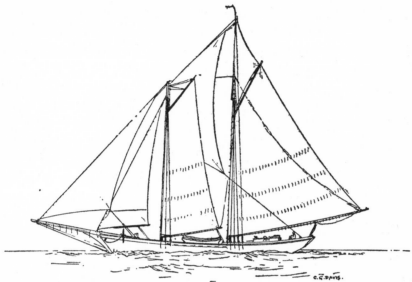

A GLOUCESTERMAN OF ABOUT *1890*

Before going on with the development of the fisherman, it is worth while to describe the painting of these vessels during the early 1880's. The majority of these schooners were painted a bottle or emerald green from water line to waist, the bulwarks above the waist being black and the cove-bead yellow; the underbody was red copper. On deck, the schooners were usually "dolled up" like the proverbial "little red wagon"; the waterways were blue or chocolate, and large circles were swept in at the foremast bed, at the great beam and at the quarters, the rest of the deck being usually gray, oil or buff. The inboard face of the bulwark stanchions was bright, and the sides were either white or cherry stain; the bottoms were painted with the waterway color. Between the stanchions, the inside of the bulwarks were cherry stained. The tops of hatches and trunk

85

were the same as the waterways. The tops of the main and quarter deck rail caps were often bright, and the sides white. Hatch coamings were either white or gray. Spars were varnished, the masthead was white, as was the bowsprit outside the stem, with the inboard portion black; but if a spike bowsprit was fitted, the whole stick was black. This scheme of painting lasted until about 1894.

The *Phillips* was not followed in hull design by any similar vessel, for in 1889 a new and more taking Burgess design came out. This was the great *Fredonia,* built by Moses Adams, at Essex, for J. Malcolm Forbes of Boston. A sister schooner with slight alterations was also laid down by Adams in a sub-contractor's yard at East Boston for Thomas F. McManus, also of Boston, who was later to become one of the greatest designers of fishing schooners. This last was the *Nellie Dixon.* Of the two, the *Dixon* was the first to join the fishing fleet, the *Fredonia* being used as a yacht for a year or so. With their graceful clipper stems, rockered keels, easy lines, and speed and handiness, these two schooners were so much admired that the majority of the new vessels following them from the stocks followed them in model. A number of vessels were built from the *Fredonia* molds, and the modelers, such as "Mel" (George M.) McClain, of Rockport, Tom Irving, of Gloucester, and Burnham, and Tarr, of Essex, got out designs incorporating many of her features. The *Fredonia* was 109.44 tons net, 99.6 feet long, 23.6 feet beam and 10.3 depth of hold. She foundered on the Banks on December 18, 1896. She introduced no really new features, but represented a refinement of the *Phillips* in a more cutaway forefoot and shorter bowsprit. It is probable that her popularity over the *Phillips* was largely due to her beauty and to the publicity she received on her initial appearance.

One of the points raised against the *Fredonia's* model was the lack of carrying capacity in relation to her length, so the modelers attempted to improve on the model in this feature, at least. Irving and McClain both turned out schooners that acquired great reputations for speed and power. Though they followed the appearance of the *Fredonia* above the water line in a general way, they did not indulge in slavish copying, but departed boldly from the original,

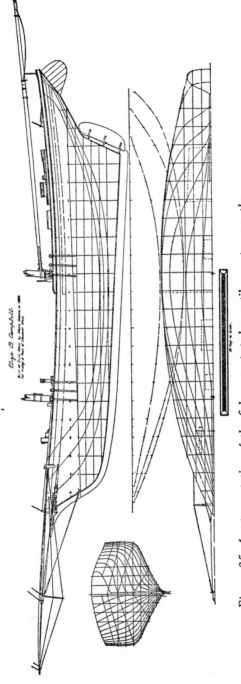

Figure 25. A representative of the fisherman popular until recent years, the
ELIZA B. CAMPBELL, 1890

working out improvements that seemed desirable. The result was that by 1890 they had developed a type that was popular until recent years. The McClain vessels may be taken as illustrations of the new model thus produced. From McClain's models were built such fine schooners as the *Eliza B. Campbell,* in 1890, the *Marguerite Haskins,* in 1893, and *M. Madaleine,* in 1894. McClain had been modeling since 1880, and had acquired a reputation with some of his early bankers, especially with the *Puritan,* in 1887.

The plan of the *Eliza B. Campbell,* Figure 25, shows the features of the class of schooners under discussion. She was built at Essex by Moses Adams for Hodge and Poole, of Gloucester, and measured 95.17 tons net, 88.4 feet long, 23.9 feet beam, and 9.8 feet depth of hold. She was lost in 1901.

The *Campbell* was one of the last vessels built with jibbooms; she had a rather complicated head rigging, using not only whiskers but also the spreader introduced with spike bowsprits. Vessels with this rig were built as late as 1894, but, as a rule, schooners built from 1890 on had the pole bowsprit.

A comparison of the four plans published here, Figures 22, 23, 24 and 25, will show the development that took place during the period we have covered, but the changes that took place in the bows and sterns of fishermen require special mention. In larger vessels the type of stem seen in the *Fears,* with the upper head rail added, gradually went out of use during the early 1880.'s. The wooden head rails were replaced by iron rods as braces to the cutwater, and the stem or cutwater knee was greatly shortened. At the same time, the cheek knees seem to have been omitted, leaving only the "noble wood" (pad at the hawse) and the trail boards. In the late 1880's, the bottom edge of the trail was rounded up at its after end to meet the after edge of the "noble wood." The result was an effect somewhat like the well-known head of the yacht *America.* The wooden catheads were retained, their bottoms being rounded off just below the waist line. It was during the development of this type of cutwater that the plumb or straight stem, such as that of the *Story,* became popular, at first retaining the "noble wood," but dropping it when bowsprit spreaders were introduced through the bows, as in the *Carrie E. Phillips*. Neither the *America* nor the plumb stems had a long popularity, both giving way to the bald clipper stem of the 1890's. This stem was merely the old "gammon knee" head, usually having an eagle head or a billet at the fore end, with no trails, the scrolls being cut into the knee and planking. The bowsprit spreaders went out of use because they were not required with the short bowsprits made possible with the cutaway forefoot that became general in the new schooners of the last of the nineties.

There was a somewhat similar evolution in the counters of these vessels. The short, wide counter sterns of the 1870's gave way to the longer overhang of the 1880's, which, for a few years, had much competition for popular favor from the deep "V" transom of the pilot boats. Finally, the overhang having retained supremacy, it was gradually lengthened during this period of its development. During the era of the Burgess schooners, the tendency was toward rather short counters with no visible knuckle at the junction of transom and horn timber, but in the 1890's, the transom was set with less rake, in the manner now popular.

Beginning in the last of the eighties and during the following twenty years, the New England fishing schooner reached its highest development; the fleet was one of which any nation might well be proud.

Chapter Seven

⚓

THE GLOUCESTER SCHOONER : III

THE GLOUCESTER SCHOONER: III

THE building of clipper bow fishing schooners continued well into the twentieth century. As an example of one of the last of this class, we have in Figure 26 the lines of the handsome *Gertrude,* built at Essex in 1902 by A. D. Story for F. J. O'Hara & Co., of Boston. The *Gertrude* measured 84.63 gross tons and 56.85 net; her registered dimensions being: length 88 feet, beam 23.4 feet and depth 9.2 feet. Built from a model by Mel McClain, her striking features were her yacht-like form and comparatively light displacement for a commercial schooner. Her easy lines, graceful ends and cutaway underbody make an attractive vessel; her long and well-shaped run, a fast one. Like many of the schooners built from half-models, her sheer was rather straight. The small displacement was undoubtedly the result of the desire for speed, but the general reduction in cargo capacity seen in most of the fishing schooners of her time was brought about by a change in the fishing industry.

After 1890, there was little or no salt banking by either Gloucester or Boston fishermen, due, perhaps, to a decreasing demand for this commodity as a result of the spread of cold storage facilities. At any rate, the need for bulky schooners of the Grand Banker class ceased and few were built after this date. Salt fish were obtained, when in demand, by sending schooners to Nova Scotia, and the large schooners were occasionally so employed. In spite of the dis-Georges as well as on the Maritime Provinces voyage, and could be of less capacity than formerly. Hence, schooners were built to continuance of banking, large schooners could be employed on the fulfill the requirements of all types of fishery. The *Gertrude* repre-

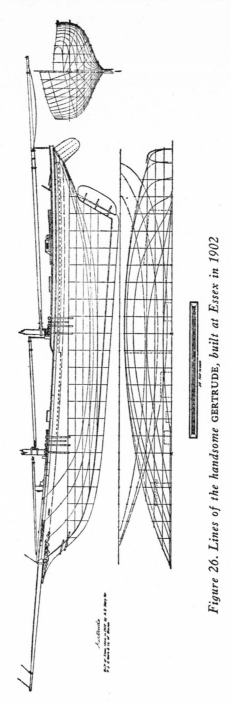

Figure 26. Lines of the handsome GERTRUDE, *built at Essex in 1902*

sents the class of schooners popular under these conditions. She was the culmination in design of the *Fredonia* type, introduced by Edward Burgess, as told in the preceding chapter. Undoubtedly, the search for speed had caused the reduction of displacement to be carried to extremes; there was a reaction toward vessels of greater capacity, as will be shown.

Figure 27 is the sail and rigging plan of the *Gertrude,* and shows, in a general way, the proportion of spars and rig popular in

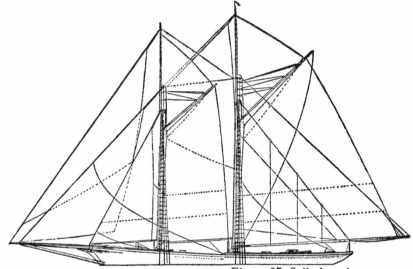

Figure 27. Sail plan of GERTRUDE

her day. Though the sail area is large, the rig is not excessive in height. The bowsprit, though long as judged by modern standards, was much shorter and lighter than formerly. As a result, the complicated head rigging used on earlier schooners could be omitted, and bowsprit spreaders were no longer seen. One characteristic, nearly always to be seen in fishing schooners, may be seen here; the masts, though stepped with some rake aft, are stayed well forward, as are also the topmasts. This was done even on new schooners. The bowsprits were usually hogged down as well.

One of the very last of the clipper bow fishermen built at Essex was the racer *Arthur James,* built from a half-model used, in 1903, to build the *Avalon*. The *Arthur James* was built by Tarr and James in 1905 and was about three feet longer than *Avalon*. McClain was responsible for this design also. Another well-known racer of this type, which is still afloat, is the *Philip P. Manta,* built in 1902. She is about the size of the *Gertrude* and is a beautiful schooner. In appearance, these boats differed little from the lines shown in Figure 26.

During the last years of the nineteenth century, fishing schooners came under the influence of that remarkable designer, Thomas F. McManus. The son of a Boston sailmaker, McManus was a well-known Boston fish buyer and also a yachtsman. During his youth he was friendly with both Dennison J. Lawlor and Edward Burgess; this, perhaps, caused him to take up the designing of fishermen as a hobby. The first built to his design were the sister ships *James S. Steele* and *Richard C. Steele,* launched in 1892. These schooners were cut away forward much more than was then common; in fact, the profile was much like that of the famous Herreshoff sloop *Gloriana,* though McManus then knew nothing of this yacht. These schooners were quite successful and were followed by a few similar vessels, but it was not until nearly 1900, when the Boston and South Shore fishing fleet was built up, that McManus's influence became apparent. The first characteristic that he introduced in his schooners at that time was the modern curved stem, now so common in the fleet. The first to have this stem were some small vessels named after Indian chiefs; hence, this type of stem soon became known at Essex and Gloucester as the "Indian head," and the schooners so built, as "Indian headers." About this time, McManus began to make a business of schooner design, to the exclusion of his fish business.

The earlier "Indian headers" had a keel line that curved from stem to sternpost. However, this made a vessel hard to haul on the marine railways because of the difficulty in setting the keel blocks. About 1902, Crowninshield, well-known Boston yacht designer, turned out some fishing schooners with short, straight keels, two examples of which were the *Stranger* and the *Harmony,* of the Boston fleet. This feature proved so successful that it was soon widely used; in fact, this form is now usually referred to as the

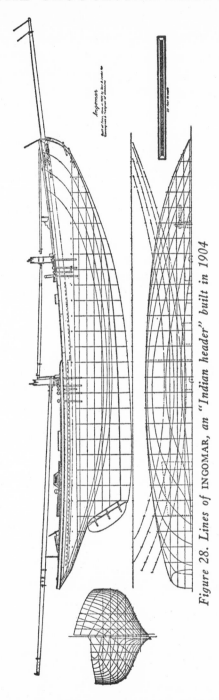

Figure 28. Lines of INGOMAR, *an "Indian header" built in 1904*

"fisherman's profile." The later "Indian headers" had this under-body profile; the famous *Elsie,* which first represented Gloucester in the Fisherman's Race, and many others, were so designed.

The "Indian headers" became very popular, first with the Boston fishermen, then at Gloucester. As a result, a great many fine schooners of this class were built during the early years of the twentieth century, including such vessels as the *Flora S. Nickerson,* and *Emily Cooney,* built in 1902, and the *Ingomar,* built in 1904. As an example of the "Indian headers," the *Ingomar,* shown in Figure 28, represents the early schooners of this class. She was built by Tarr and James at Essex during the winter of 1903-4, and was of 143.36 gross, and 103.58 net tons. Her registered dimensions were: length, 104.8 feet; beam 25.7 feet and depth 11.4 feet. A study of her lines will show many characteristics of the McManus design, particularly the shape of the midsection, an important feature. Its shape gave an easy roller, and a vessel that was, as a result, easy on her gear, as well as a good carrier. *Elsie* had practically the same midsection. Speed was obtained by well-shaped ends, and the long and rather flat buttocks which are noticeable features of all McManus' fast schooners. Another feature is the rather marked trim by the head to be seen in most of them. It is claimed by the fishermen that this improves the sailing of their vessels, but this is open to doubt, as they invariably trim them by the head even before they go off on their trials. Hence, they do not know whether their assumption applies to an individual vessel or not; this is proved by the fact that they have ruined the sailing of some of the racing fishermen by such trim. Certainly, there is nothing in the lines of the majority of fishing schooners built at Essex that warrants the belief that such trim is best. The *Ingomar* went ashore during the winter of 1935-36 and was a total loss.

The rig of the "Indian headers" varied little or not at all from that of the *Gertrude,* unless in a slight increase in proportional height. The spar dimensions of the *Ingomar,* as given the spar-maker, were: mainmast, deck to cap, 77 feet; total length, 88'-6", diameter, 18 inches; foremast, deck to cap, 68'-10"; total length, 78'-6", diameter, 18 inches; mainmast head, 11 feet; foremast head,

10 feet; bowsprit, 29'-6" outboard, 15½ inches diameter; main boom, 75 feet long, 13 inches diameter; main gaff, 44'-3" long, 10½ inches diameter; fore gaff, 29'-6" long, 9 inches diameter; fore boom, 29'-6" long, 8½ inches diameter; fore topmast, 42 feet long, 10¼ inches diameter; maintopmast, 47 feet long, 10¾ inches diameter; and jumbo boom (forestaysail boom), 27 feet long, 6 inches diameter.

A KNOCKABOUT FISHERMAN OF *1902*

Schooners of the *Ingomar* type were built until recently, the *L. A. Dunton,* one of this class, being built as late as 1921. Except for variation in size and in the use of the straight keel already mentioned, most of the McManus schooners were similar to the *Ingomar,* though a few were designed with a somewhat longer bow overhang.

McManus was responsible for still another innovation. He had noticed, in strolling about the wharves, that the footropes on the bowsprits of many fishing schooners were in bad shape. Many men had been lost as a result of carelessness in this matter, but it was hard to get fishermen to take proper care of such gear. Then, too, men were often washed off the bowsprit in heavy weather even when the gear was good. Altogether, it seemed that the bowsprit was not wholly desirable in a fishing schooner, since it was also a source of trouble in maneuvering about the wharves. These observations led McManus to design a schooner, without this spar, which he thought would be as handy and safe as the small sloops then becoming popular among Massachusetts Bay yachtsmen. However, he found it very difficult to interest fishermen in schooners of this type. In spite of every argument, and even the exhibition of the half-model of the proposed schooner in Boston, it was some time before McManus found anyone willing to risk his money in such a vessel. At last, in the fall of 1901, Captain Wm. Thomas, of Portland, and Cassius Hunt, were prevailed upon to try the new design. Oxner and Story, of Essex, were commissioned to build a schooner of this design that winter, to be named the *Helen B. Thomas*. So it was that the first "knockabout" fishing schooner was launched in the spring of 1902. The new vessel was peculiar in design and appearance, having a short, straight keel with much drag, and a small mid-section, also seeming to be a smaller schooner drawn out forward to where the end of the bowsprit would be in an ordinary rig. This gave her a lot of freeboard forward as well as quite a bit of sheer. When brought to sailing trim, however, the *Thomas* was a fine-looking ship and, after some fishing and racing, the fishermen were willing to admit that she was practical. In one of her races, she met the slippery *Philip P. Manta* with success. The *Helen B. Thomas* measured 76.99 gross and 48.19 net tons, her registered dimensions being: length, 94.2 feet; beam, 21.6 feet and depth, 9.2 feet. Her success naturally led to others of the same rig being built.

The next "knockabout" to be built was that exceptional sailer, the *Shepherd King* which, strangely enough, was not a McManus design. The *Shepherd King* was constructed by the builders of the *Helen B. Thomas* at Essex in 1904, from a half-model made by one of the firm, Oxner, as an improvement on the first knockabout. Captain J. O. Brigham, one of her owners, had many of his ideas incorporated in this schooner, among which were a more burden-

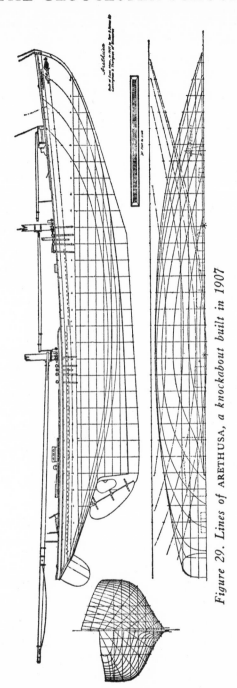

Figure 29. Lines of ARETHUSA, a knockabout built in 1907

some midsection, very straight sheer, longer keel and short over-hangs. The new vessel was also given a catboat bow with a short overhang, the stemhead falling inboard at the top. Somewhat larger than the *Thomas,* the *Shepherd King* was at her best in a breeze and had a great reputation, not only for speed in heavy weather

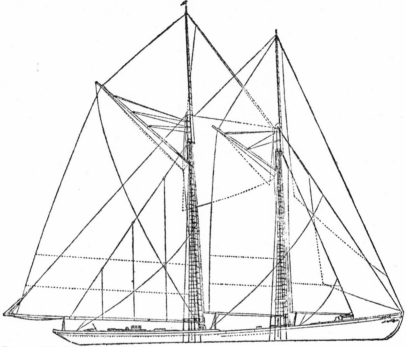

Figure 30. Sail plan of ARETHUSA

but also for seaworthiness. In Gloucester parlance, she was "a dog — she'd follow you anywhere."

After 1906, a number of the "knockabouts" were built, many of them large and very fast. However, there was one objection to this type, and this affected later designs. The builders had always fixed the price of a new schooner on the over all length; hence, the owner of a knockabout had to pay for the long overhangs first used on this type. Yet such a vessel as the *Helen B. Thomas* had less room and cargo capacity than an ordinary schooner of her length, mak-

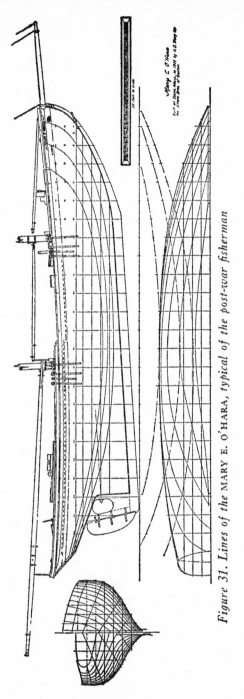

Figure 31. Lines of the MARY E. O'HARA, typical of the post-war fisherman

ing the knockabout an expensive type to build in relation to her capacity. This objection was overcome by shortening and deepening the bow overhang. This, in turn, caused the later knockabouts to have a high narrow rig in order to get the proper balance.

As an example of an improved knockabout of the more modern design, Figure 28 shows the lines of the famous and beautiful *Arethusa,* built at Essex in 1907 by Tarr and James for Cunningham & Thompson, of Gloucester, from a design by McManus. She was intended to be the largest knockabout that was practical in a fisherman, and is still the largest ever built at Essex. She measured 157 gross and 107 net tons, her registered dimensions being: length, 114 feet; beam, 25.6 feet and depth, 12.5 feet. The *Arethusa's* maiden trip was to Newfoundland for frozen herring, in November, 1907. The next spring she was caught poaching in Canadian waters and was pursued by a Canadian cutter, but escaped. Later, she had a similar experience, escaping from the Canadian cutter *Fiona* by her sailing. In 1913, the *Arethusa* went ashore on Sable Island but got off again, a most unusual feat.

After the usual run of adventures common to the fishing industry, the *Arethusa* was bought by Captain Bill McCoy in 1921 for a rum runner. Painted white, and fitted with a short bowsprit (17 feet outboard), with the name *Tomoka* on her bows, she was one of the most daring and notorious of the ships in "Rum Row."

The praise that McCoy lavished on his schooner can be appreciated by study of the lines shown in Figure 29. Power and beauty are combined with capacity and speed. It has been said that it is easy to design a fast fisherman as compared to the problem of designing one that combines both speed and capacity.

Figure 30 is the sail and rigging plan of the *Arethusa,* and shows the characteristics of the knockabout fisherman rig and spar proportions, including, also, such typical details as the gallows for the fore or "jumbo" stay and the arrangement of the headstays.

Motors were installed in fishing schooners early in the century and steam auxiliary power was tried out much earlier. However, it was not until about 1910 that large power was tried and it was not until the war that such power became common. During and after the war, schooners were built with large power plants, like the *Mary E. O'Hara,* shown in Figure 31. This vessel was built at Essex in 1921-22 by A. D. Story for the O'Hara Brothers of Boston, and measured 108 gross and 49 net tons. Her registered dimensions were: length, 92 feet; beam, 22.8 feet; and depth 11 feet. Though not a particularly handsome schooner, the *O'Hara* is well liked and generally satisfactory under present conditions. She is now little more than a power boat.

A number of schooners similar to the O'Hara have been built in Maine but the out-and-out power boat was the most popular type previous to the present period of depression in the fisheries.

Chapter Eight

⚓

GLOUCESTER "SLOOP BOATS"

GLOUCESTER "SLOOP BOATS"

IN SPITE of the fact that the Gloucester fishing schooners are well known to all yachtsmen, the fishing sloops of the same port are rarely mentioned. These sloops were among the largest seagoing vessels of this rig employed on our coasts. They were fast and seaworthy and, of equal importance to the fisherman, they were good carriers for their size. Their length ranged all the way from 40 to 60 feet over all, but the popular size was about 50 feet. Usually, they had short quarter decks with the cabin trunk aft. This was not universal, however, as some had flush decks and some had the trunk forward. The smaller boats were but little different from the Friendship sloops of Maine; in fact, some of these were purchased by the Gloucestermen. The larger sloops were practically miniature fishing schooners in hull. The type has now almost disappeared, having been replaced by power boats, so that it is time that they be recorded.

The history of the sloop in the fishing trade reaches back to colonial days. Sloops were employed in all trades along our coasts from somewhere around 1700 to about 1795, by which time the schooner had very nearly driven the older rig out of the larger craft. Occasionally, some of these large sloops were used for fishing in the North Atlantic. Certain ports seem to have owned more sloops than others. Scituate, Charlestown, Boston, Salem, Beverly, Gloucester and Newburyport, all had rather large fleets of vessels with this rig during colonial days. However, it is probable that few or none of these boats were built for the fishing business alone; rather they were built for general purposes, and were used as fishermen only when it was profitable so to employ them. At other times they were traders, coasters, packets or produce boats.

In type, the early sloops were full-ended craft, having a somewhat barrel-shaped midsection and some drag to the keel. The sloop rig then popular differed much from the rig as we now know it, as it had square topsails and a square course as well as two or three headsails and a gaff mainsail, loose-footed. Such vessels were more carriers than clippers, and were rarely over 60 feet in length. These boats, and their successors, the modern gaff-topsail sloops, were, in turn, occasionally used as fishing vessels, particularly in the shore and market fisheries, from 1800 on. None the less, the sloop rig was neither numerous nor popular in the fishing fleet during the period of the Chebacco boat and pinky (1800-1850), as these types fulfilled the requirements of the fishermen far better than the contemporary sloops.

The first real impetus which the sloop rig received in the fishing fleet came in the 50's and 60's of the last century. A large number of Irish fishermen, many of whom were from County Galway, settled in or near Boston during this period. These men had been brought up in the "Galway hooker," one of the few Irish types of sailing craft. The "hooker" was a small, cutter-rigged boat, about 35 feet long and 11'-3" beam, drawing 5'-8" of water, loaded. These boats were full-bowed, with low, round floors and some drag to the keel; they were rather good sailers, though crude in build and rig. Their rig was that of a bald-headed cutter with two headsails. The Irish built a few of these at Boston, and American builders, when similar boats were ordered, improved on the type. The so-called "Boston cutter" or "Irish boat" was the result. These boats had the same rig as that of the "hooker," but the hull was quite different, having more deadrise and sharper lines. The "Boston cutter" was not particularly handsome, having a nearly vertical stem and a heart-shaped transom, also set nearly upright, combined with too little sheer. However, they were good sailers and were popular with the Boston Irish. Eventually they became very common in Massachusetts Bay and so were well known to the Gloucestermen, particularly after the Civil War.

GLOUCESTER "SLOOP BOATS"

The Gloucestermen had replaced their pinkies with larger schooners during the 50's, a period of great prosperity in the fishing business, except for the last three years of the decade. During the 40's, the method of selling fish had changed; the old way of selling direct to marketmen, or peddlers, was replaced by wholesale selling through auction. Open bidding made the daily fluctuation of prices much wider, and the middlemen created by wholesale buying usually paid the highest prices to the first arrivals on certain days.

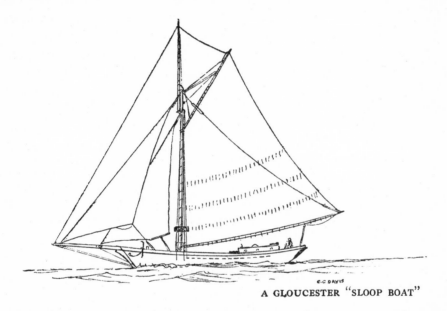

A GLOUCESTER "SLOOP BOAT"

This condition made speed in the fishing vessels a necessity. The large schooners of the 50's and 60's were the result of the need of speed, but the great financial depression of the early 70's gave this class of vessel a great setback. The depression was followed by the ruinous Canadian Treaty, and by other blows to the fishing industry, the result being the financial ruin of many schooner owners and the slump in the building of new vessels of this class. Therefore, many fishermen turned to the sloops, some of the Gloucestermen buying "Boston cutters." The Gloucestermen, however, had an aversion towards the Boston boats, preferring Essex-built craft.

Hence the Essex designers developed another type of sloop, which soon became popular as it was found that very small schooners were not fast enough to compete with sloops.

During the 1880's, the sloops, or rather, to give the boats their local name, "sloop boats," became rather popular, particularly in the 'longshore and market fisheries. The years between 1880 and 1907 saw the rise and fall of the "sloop boats" in the Gloucester fleet. The first sloops built at Essex, and those built afterwards at Gloucester, differed greatly from the earlier Boston boats. The "sloop boats" were sharper-ended and had more deadrise and some hollow in the garboards; also, they had counters. The new type was variously known as "Essex sloop boat," "Gloucester sloop boat" or "Salem sloop boat." On Cape Ann, "sloop boat" was a term applied to sloops smaller in size than the standard fishing schooner. A similar term was applied to small schooners, *ie.,* "schooner boats." In other words, the addition of "boat" to the name of the rig was the diminutive of "sloop" or "schooner." Eventually, "sloop boat" was applied to all sloops, through usage.

Though the first "sloop boats" were built at Essex, nearly all those built after 1882 were laid down at Gloucester. As a rule, they were built during the slack season, when the builder desired to keep his gangs intact; usually this was during the summer. As a result, most of these boats were built on speculation and kept in the yards in an unfinished state until sold. In Gloucester, most of the owners of this type were Americans and Portuguese, while in Boston they were usually Irish. Many owners of large fleets of fishing schooners began their careers as sloop boatmen. The "sloop boats" replaced the "Boston cutter" in the Boston fleet during the 80's.

While nearly all of the Gloucester, and some of the Essex builders put up "sloop boats," the majority were built at Gloucester by Thomas A. Irving and by the Bishop brothers, John and Hugh, both of whom had yards. Tom Irving modeled most of the "sloop boats"; in fact, fully 90 percent were from half models made by him between 1890 to 1906. Irving was not only a fine carpenter but an excellent designer as well. He built many sloops and schooners on his own account and at times was employed as foreman by the

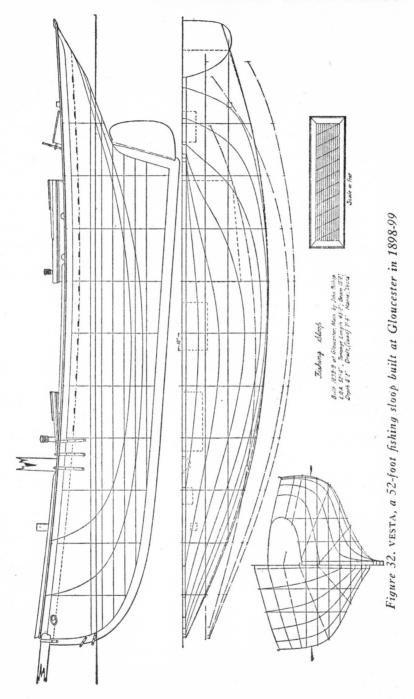

Fishing Sloop

Built 1898-9 at Gloucester, Mass. by John Bishop
L.O.A. 52'-6"; Tonnage Length 43'7"; Beam 15'0";
Depth 6'2" Draft, (aext) 7'4" Name: Vesta

Scale in feet

Figure 32. VESTA, a 52-foot fishing sloop built at Gloucester in 1898-99

other builders. The Bishops may have modeled sloops and schooners. As their vessels were marked by unusually long counters, seen in the work of none of the other builders, it seems reasonable to conclude that at least one of the brothers did some modeling. Most of their vessels were from models made by others, however, many of which were Irving's work.

It is difficult to decide how much the "sloop boats" were influenced by contemporary yachts. At first glance, these boats look very much like the clipper-bowed cutter yachts of the late 80's. However, their hull form and proportions differed greatly from those of the yachts. The Gloucester sloops were more like the large fishing schooners in hull form. The effect of the designs of yacht architects on the fishing fleet has been much overrated and their influence is more apparent than real. The most successful of the designs have been those that followed the type developed by the Essex modelers most closely, though the fishing schooners designed by Edward Burgess were excellent examples of well-proportioned designs.

The Essex modelers were rule-of-thumb designers, yet their work was on a par with that of contemporary yacht designers. The explanation lies in the manner in which each class developed — the fisherman through a long process of trial and error, while yachts are molded by fashion, theory and racing rules. In the latter type of boat, theory was too often contrary to fact, and the effect of racing rules has been admittedly a handicap to advance in yacht design. The modelers of fishing schooners and sloops, however, were influenced by the requirements of the trade, and to a minor extent by the prejudices of the fishermen. The demand for speed, combined with seaworthiness and capacity, ruled the design of fishermen from 1850 to the time of the introduction of the power boat.

Figure 32 shows the lines of a flush-decked, plumb-stemmed "sloop boat" built at Gloucester during the winter of 1898-99, by John Bishop. Her name was the *Vesta*. Archer Poland, the Essex loftsman, laid her down in September, 1898. I have been unable to discover who made her half-model, but as she has the long counter mentioned earlier she may be the design of one of the Bishops. In some ways she is reminiscent of the Boston pilot schooners and of

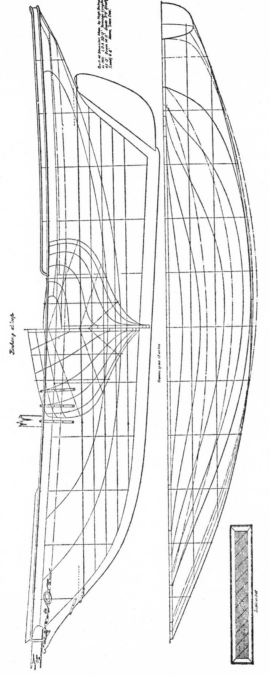

Figure 33. The LAURA ENOS, *built in 1901, represents the type popular at the beginning of the century*

the plumb-stemmed fishing schooners designed by Dennison J. Lawlor. In spite of her sharp ends, the full midsection gave good carrying capacity while its shape gave initial stability. The hull form is indicative of great speed reaching and running, while the sharp entrance and large lateral plane, combined with depth, must have made this sloop a good performer to windward. The hull is a form that would move through the water with little fuss, and would require little power to drive, considering the large displacement. This model has been universally admired, and apparently earlier sloops were built from it, judging by the dimensions of sloops given in the enrollments in the Gloucester custom-house. While such identification is doubtful, still, the model appears to have been made about 1890, and is representative of the earlier sloops of that period.

The deck arrangement is more or less typical of the "sloop boats." At the stern there is a wheelbox, with quarter bitts on each side, forward of which, in the other named, are the cabin trunk, the main hatch, the forecacstle companionway, mainmast, forepeak hatch, windlass and riding bitts. Some sloops had two hatches amidships, both on the centerline. Occasionally the forecastle companionway was forward of the mast. If the boat was used for trawling, the thrawling winch was usually forward of the mast. Most boats had a break in the deck just forward of the trunk. Some of the smaller boats had the trunk forward, the mast passing through its roof in some of these.

Figure 33 shows a smaller boat built by Hugh Bishop, a brother of John, at Gloucester, in 1901. This boat was modeled by Tom Irving and had a short quarter deck, in the manner usual in these craft. The name of this sloop was the *Laura Enos;* she represents the type that was popular at the beginning of the present century. The size of boat shown was the most common in the 'longshore fisheries. The changes in hull form that took place in the fishing fleet between the time of the building of the *Vesta* and of the *Laura Enos* are plain in the lines of these two boats. The *Enos* had a more marked hollow in her garboards and a more cutaway forefoot than had the *Vesta,* as well as more beam in proportion to length, and harder bilges.

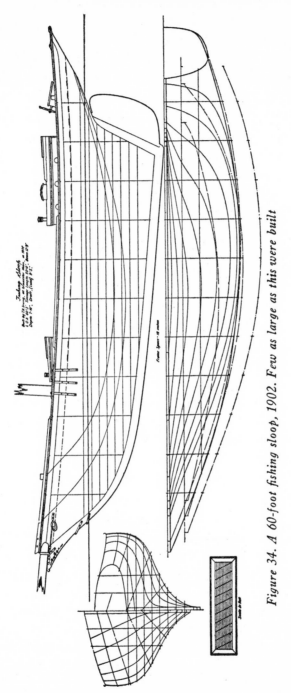

Figure 34. A 60-foot fishing sloop, 1902. Few as large as this were built

The last two items, however, were due to the smaller size of the *Enos* and, hence, her need for greater relative stability, rather than to a change in hull form in the fleet. It must be added, however, that Irving's models usually show more hollow in the garboards and harder bilges than do the models by contemporary designers. The *Enos* had a somewhat narrower transom than was usual; her sheer, like that most of Irving's models, was rather straight.

Figure 34, shows the lines of a larger "sloop boat" by the same modeler, built at Gloucester in 1902. This boat was of the largest class of sloop-rigged fishing boats on our coasts. Few as large were built at Gloucester or Essex and fewer yet were for the local fleet, as the Gloucestermen preferred the schooner rig in such large hulls. I have been unable to identify this sloop or to find the name of her builder for a certainty, but I think she was built by Irving for Boston parties. So large a flush-decked vessel was unusual in the fishing fleet. It is an interesting fact that some "schooner boats" were built on the same general model. All these sloops have one feature in common, their long run with rather straight buttocks. Most of them trimmed more by the stern than the plans indicate, which made the free board at the bow greater than shown. Some had more outside keel, 12 to 14 inches being the most common amount.

The construction was of the usual fisherman type. Sawn frames, spaced 17 or 18 inches, were employed. The planking was about 1½ inches thick, with 2-inch fender strakes. Timbers, keel, keelson, were of white oak; planking was usually of pine. The decking was of white pine, oiled. The ceiling was of pine and hardwood. Fastenings were galvanized iron and locust "trunnels." In general, the construction of the "sloop boats" was the same as that of the fishing schooners, except for reduced scantlings.

The arrangement below was on the same plan as that of a fishing schooner. The cabin, aft, contained two to four berths, lockers and a heating stove; amidships was the fish hold. Some sloops, built for owners at other ports than Gloucester, had fish wells. Forward was the forecastle, containing from four to twelve berths, according to the size of the vessel, and the galley.

The large sloops carried as many as eight dories, nested on each side of the main hatch, amidships. The number was subject to the kind of fishing done, of course. This consideration also had some effect on the deck arrangement, particularly on the location of the forecastle companionway. The finish above and below deck was strong, cheap and practical, rather than handsome. The ballast was

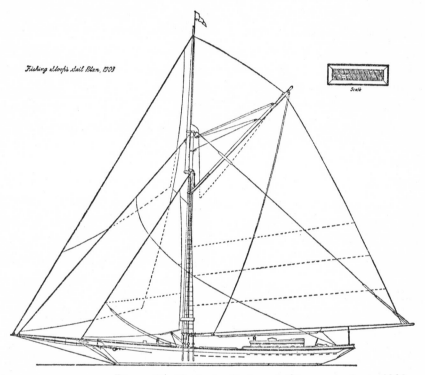

Figure 35. Typical sail plan of Gloucester sloop, 1903

all inside, and consisted of concrete and loose stones or gravel, some scrap iron white or gray trunk and hatches; the inside of the bulwarks was gray also. The railcap was usually white, or finished in oil. The waist line, about halfway up the bulwarks on the outside of the hull, was set off by a gold stripe; this was an inch or so below the waist line and above the scuppers so as not to be stained by the drainings of the deck.

AMERICAN SAILING CRAFT

A few centerboard sloops were employed in the fisheries, most of which were owned at Salem. I found the lines of but one; she differed but little from a sloop yacht of the late 70's or early 80's. These boats were neither numerous nor highly developed, and hardly constitute a type.

The rig of the 'sloop boats" was that of the American modification of the English cutter of the late 80's. The sails carried were a forestaysail, jib, jib topsail, gaff mainsail and gaff topsail. The difference between the rigs of the cutter and "sloop boat" lies in the spars, the bowsprit of the sloop being fixed instead of running, and the mast being farther forward than the cutter's. The sail plan shown, Figure 35, is representative of the rig of the "sloop boat." The spar proportions varied somewhat among the different builders. When auxiliary engines were introduced, the rigs were much reduced in size and topmasts were rarely fitted. The details of standing and running rigging were the same as those of contemporary fishing schooners. The early sloops had hemp rigging throughout; wire standing rigging was introduced in these boats in the early 90's. The large rigs were necessary to drive the heavy displacement hulls, but there was no difficulty in handling as the crews were large. All gear was much stronger and heavier than that of a yacht of similar size.

About 1906, the power boat began to replace the out-and-out sailing sloops and schooners (the first gasoline auxiliary was launched in 1903), and from then on the sloops were sold out of Massachusetts waters very rapidly. Because the reputation of the "sloop boats" was so well known, the boats in good condition were in great demand. Unfortunately, few of these sloops were bought by yachtsmen, as the type of yacht then fashionable was markedly different from the fishing sloop. It will be recalled that the first decade of the present century was the period of popularity of the "fast cruiser" of extreme proportions and design, the result of the old "length and sail area" rule. At the present time few of the "sloop boats" are to be found on Massachusetts Bay. Only one is used as a fishing boat at Gloucester, and another is employed as a yacht.

GLOUCESTER "SLOOP BOATS"

The "sloop boat" influenced the well-known Friendship sloops, and now we see a trend towards a similar type in yacht design. It would seem that a sloop on lines similar to the type under discussion would make a satisfactory deep-water racer, if the performance of such heavy boats as *Jolie Brise* is any criterion.

Chapter Nine

⚓

THE PINKIES

Chapter Nine

⚓

THE PINKIES

THE double-ender, in numerous forms, is a very popular type of seagoing sailing yacht. Many foreign types, such as the Scandinavian double-enders, have been utilized by our designers in their search for extreme seaworthiness. Strangely enough, in spite of the popularity of the Scandinavian designs, one rarely sees an example of the many American types of double-ender in our yachting fleet. This situation appears to be due to lack of information rather than to shortcomings in our national types. It must be remembered that our double-enders were evolved through a long process of trial and error, to suit the conditions of wind and water met on our coasts. It is logical to assume that our types, thus developed, are therefore more suitable for our use than are foreign types evolved for different conditions.

When double-enders are under discussion, one of the first that comes to mind is the old New England pinky. These craft are well known in a general way, but the details of their hull design are not so familiar, nor are the different types of pinky recognizable to most of us. This the explanation, perhaps, for the lack of copies and adaptations in our fleets.

There is little doubt that the importance of the sharp stern, as a feature in the design of seaworthy sailing craft, has been overly stressed. It is possible to design an equally seaworthy boat with other forms of stern. However, the sharp stern possesses certain advantages; it is cheap to build, and perfect longitudinal balance of hull under seagoing conditions is more easily obtained by its use. This last gives greater comfort in rough water. The objections are mainly a loss of initial stability, due to the lack of bearings aft, and the curtailing of deck space and of room below deck. These objections may be largely overcome by proper design. In the final analysis, the choice of stern form is one of personal opinion and preference.

An attempt to trace the ancestry of the pinkies is unsatisfactory, due to the almost total lack of written records pertaining to the subject. The name "pinky" is evidently the diminutive of the old shipbuilder's term "pink." The pink was a sharp-sterned vessel, with a false stern overhang somewhat similar to that of the pinky's as we know it. The pink was variously rigged. Some were ships, others were snows, brigantines, schooners, ketches and sloops. These vessels were employed in the Baltic and North Sea trades, and were probably well known to the early American colonists. Drawings of these old pinks may be found in Chapman's *Navalis Mercatoria Architecturia,* published in 1764, a copy of which is in the New York Public Library.

The early fisheries on our coasts was an incidental trade, carried on only when demand warranted the fitting out of a vessel. Hence, up until about 1800, there was no real type of offshore fishing boat. Large vessels, built for general trade, rigged as ships, snows, brigs, brigantines, ketches, sloops and schooners, were used up until this date. Soon after the Revolution, a small type of inshore fishing boat was introduced in the neighborhood of Gloucester and developed in the nearby parish of Chebacco, now the town of Essex. These craft were small double-enders, rarely exceeding 40 feet in length, rigged as "cat-schooners" (*i.e.,* a schooner without bowsprit or headsail), having also the pink stern similar to that of the later pinkies. These small boats became known as "Chebacco boats." Later on, a square-sterned hull, of similar rig and size, was introduced, a type known as the "dogbody," the reason for the name being unknown. These vessels were very small, at first, but slowly grew in size with the passing years. By 1800, they were large enough to enter the Banks fishery and became the offshore fishing type. By this time the trade had become quite important, and gave steady employment to both men and boats. After the War of 1812, the fisheries grew prosperous, and the vessels became larger, with bigger sail plans, as a result of which the Chebacco boats began to carry bowsprits, and thus became "full-rigged." While the dogbodies became merely small schooners, the Chebacco boats evolved into a separate class, which, about 1816, became known as pinkies, because of the similarity of their stern to that of the old pinks. The name pinky does not appear to have been applied to the Chebacco boats, in spite of their pink sterns. Pink-sterned schooners are mentioned in custom-house records as early as 1812, however.

These pinkies, mostly built at Essex, soon became famous for their seaworthiness and comfort in blowing weather. The pinky did not strain herself in the heavy seas of a North Atlantic gale, riding the seas like a duck. Some of the Chebacco boats and pinkies were fast in rough water, and their good qualities caused them to be widely copied along the coast. The pinky type was popular for many years and gave way only when changes in fishing methods made a larger and roomier hull necessary. The employment of dories, which became common in the forties, made the "sharpshooter" type of schooner desirable. It must be kept in mind that the pinky really played no part in the development of the fishing schooner, for schooners of the old "heeltapper" type were in use, not only in the same period as the pinky, but, also, at a much earlier date. The pinky was really a distinct type, rather than a stage in the development of the schooner.

The Essex pinky, the first of the type, became very common about 1820, and was a remarkable boat. The design embodied seaworthiness, comfort in heavy weather and good sailing qualities, combined with carrying capacity, to a remarkable degree. Full-ended, with low, rounding floors, as a rule, their lines were sweet and beautifully modeled. The boat was also perfectly balanced. The hull was round and full on deck, both fore and aft; the water lines forward were sharp and convex, while aft they were sharp and concave.

There are but two reliable sources of information on the Essex pinkies, the well-known plans of the *Eagle,* drawn by the late Martin Erismann, as taken off a pinky built at Essex in 1820, and the half-model of the pinky *July* built in 1837, which is in the U. S.

National Museum, Washington, D. C. The *Eagle* measured 47 feet over all, 12'-6" beam, and 6'-6" draft. The *July* was 52 feet over all, with beam of 14 feet, 7 feet depth, and 8 feet draft. The catalog states that her beam was 16 feet, but the model molds but 13'-7". The Essex pinky had a strong sheer, rounded forefoot, raking sternpost, strong drag to the keel and was rather deep and narrow. Most of them were fitted with a rather small rig, — jib, fore, and mainsail. In 1845, the pinky *Lorenzo Story* carried, in addition to these, a flying jib set on a jibboom and a jackyard gaff topsail. A maintopmast staysail was carried in light weather, as well. Though a fitted maintopmast was usually carried, the pinky does not appear to ever have had a foretopmast fitted.

The stern of the Essex pinky was typical of all pinky types; the bulwarks were carried well abaft the sternpost, finishing with a narrow raking transom or "tombstone," abaft the rudder head. This was high enough, due to the sheering up of the bulwarks, to act as a boom crotch. The underside of this false overhang was open, so as not to hold water. This whole structure was merely a portion of the bulwarks, and the loss of it would not affect the seaworthiness of the pinky any more than the loss of a part of the bulwarks in the case of a modern schooner. The pink stern was not put on for looks; rather, there were practical reasons for its use. The stern served to protect the helmsman and the rudder, to support the mainsheet horse, acted as a seat of ease, and was used to hang nets on, as well as for a boom crotch. This type of stern makes the sharp stern of the pinky somewhat more roomy on deck than would otherwise be the case.

Most of the Essex pinkies were built "by eye," without the aid of plans or half-models. Hence the Essex boats varied in deadrise and rake of ends, though the general proportions were about the same in every boat. The first three-masted schooner built at Essex was a pinky hull. The ordinary pinky built at Essex was between 50 and 52 feet over all, 45 and 48 feet l.w.l., 13 and 14 feet beam, 5 and 7 feet depth, and 6 to 9 feet draft. The dimensions of the pinky *Tiger,* as given by Collins, are: 52' x 48' x 13'-3" x 5', and her spars measured: bowsprit outboard, 14 feet; foremast above deck, 40 feet; fore boom, 17'-6"; fore gaff, 16'-6"; mainmast above deck, 42 feet; top-mast, 18 feet; main boom, 33 feet; main gaff, 18 feet. The masts of the pinkies raked about 10 degrees, and the bowsprits steeved somewhere around 15 degrees.

The construction of the pinky was strong and rough. The Essex boats were built of the best oak; it is said that only the heart of the white oak was used. Their frames were sawn and were double, closely spaced, with cant frames in bow and stern. There were heavy "wales" worked into the topsides, and a keelson was employed.

A PINKY

The boats were ceiled and, usually, clamps were fitted. It will be seen that these boats were very well built. Some of the pinkies had fish wells fitted, flooded by means of holes bored through the bottom; these smack-pinkies were usually employed in the lobster, or other inshore fisheries. The later pinkies were painted green from water line to thick strake or "wale," which, with the bulwarks, were tarred or painted black, set off with red, yellow, green, or white stripes. The bottom was sometimes treated with a mixture of white-wash and tallow, verdigris, or tallow and pitch. The early boats were tarred above and below the water line.

129

As a rule, the pinky steered with a tiller, though some of the last boats had crude wheels, working with blocks and tackles on deck. Their deck fittings were few and crude, and little ironwork was used. A small gammon knee head, without trailboards or headrails, constituted the stem finish. The rig of an Essex pinky was rather remarkable for its simplicity, there being little standing rigging. The cuddy was under a raised deck forward and was a dark and smoky place. A crude open fireplace supplied heat for cooking and warmth. A wooden chimney, plastered on the inside, carried off part of the smoke though some of these boats had brick chimneys. The cabin was horribly smoky. The late George S. Wesson, writing in *Old Time New England,* claimed that smoked halibut was introduced to a waiting world through the fishermen's custom of hanging portions of the halibut in the cuddy to dry, which became well smoked "due to the primitive cooking and heating arrangements of the pinky class." Mr. Lewis H. Story, of Essex, told me that the tradition was that a large number of pinkies were built miles inland, in the woods, and were hauled to the waterside by oxen. Essex became a shipbuilding center in early days by reason of the excellent stand of white oak in the neighborhood. Once the yards were established, it is natural that they continued long after the oak had disappeared.

It may well be said that, of all American fishing types, the pinky is the most seaworthy and comfortable for deep water work. The Essex pinky was dry either under way or at anchor. As long as the pinky predominated on the Banks, the loss of life and vessels was slight; they were weatherly, handy and safe under any conditions of weather. It is said that two pinkies were among the few vessels that beat out of Chaleur Bay in the terrific "American Gale" of October, 1851, when a large part of the Gloucester fleet was wiped out.

The pinky was hove-to under a double-reefed foresail with helm lashed; when this was done the crew calmly called it a day and retired to the cuddy. The pinky would not fall off, but would lay well up and, because of the excellent longitudinal balance of the hull, she would ride over the seas without any leaping and diving. Her easy motion prevented the racking and straining which often takes place

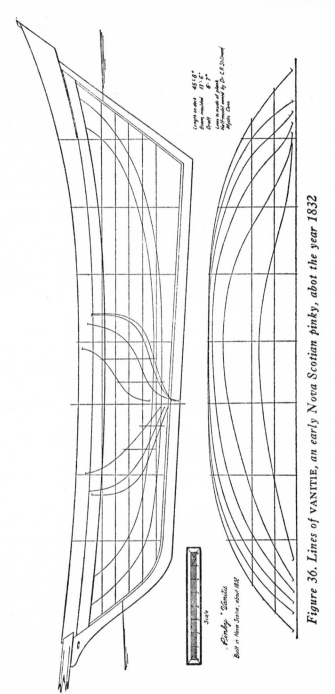

Length on deck 45'-8"
Beam moulded 13'-6"
Draft 6'-7"
Lines to scale of plank
Half-model owned by Dr C.R. Stillwent
Mystic Conn

Scale

Pinkey "Vanitie
Built in Nova Scotia, about 1832

Figure 36. Lines of VANITIE, *an early Nova Scotian pinky, abot the year 1832*

in less well-formed types. This increased the life of both hull and rig to say nothing of the effect on the comfort of the crew.

Maine builders adopted the Chebacco boat, the dogbody and the pinky in turn, ollowing the Essex builders. The Maine pinkies were on the same general model as the Essex boats, but usually the Maine pinkies had much less sheer and, often, lower bulwarks. They also had more deadrise, as a rule, though some were very full-ended. The dimensions of a typical Maine pinky, the *Trenton,* whose half-model is in the U. S. National Museum, are as follows: length over all, 47 feet; beam, 14'-2"; depth, 6'-4". The *Trenton* was built at Trenton, Maine, in 1840. Compared to the Essex-built *July,* the *Trenton* is somewhat fuller, and has more beam in proportion to length. The Maine pinkies had less external keel than had the Essex craft. The rig and fittings of the Maine pinkies were practically the same as those of the original model.

The Canadian Maritime Provinces also copied the Essex types, the dogbodies being known as "jakes," and both pinkies and "jakes" were built in this century, particularly in the Province of New Brunswick. The accompanying plan of the *Vanitie,* Figure 36, built at Yarmouth, N. S., about 1832, shows the lines of the Canadian type. Their rig and details did not vary from those of the Essex pinkies. Like the Maine type, they had more deadrise than the original model, but were also rather full-ended. It will be noticed that all the pinky types are nearly alike in size.

The fourth and most developed type of pinky was employed around Eastport, Maine, during the fifties and sixties. These pinkies, being in competition with sloops and schooners, were built to sail faster than the types just described. The Eastport pinkies were employed mostly in the herring fishery, and, while not having to work so far offshore as the Essex, and the other Maine types, they had to be good sea boats. The Eastport vessels were more of the clipper type, as will be seen.

Figure 37 shows the lines of an Eastport pinky, taken from a half-model in the possession of Mr. Reynolds Beale, of Rockport, Mass. The details are drawn from measurements of two old hulks and from pictures. The date of the half-model is unknown, but is

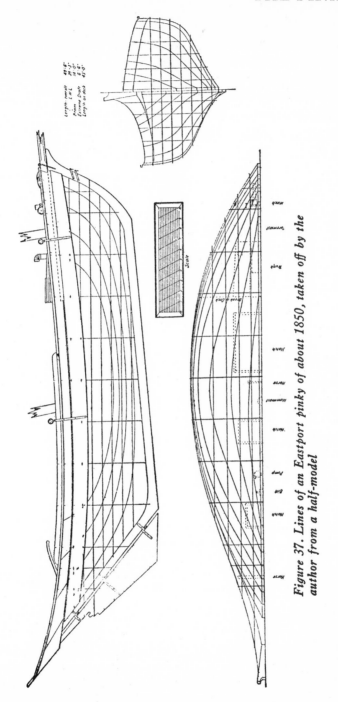

Figure 37. Lines of an Eastport pinky of about 1850, taken off by the author from a half-model

probably about 1855. The example measures 49'-6" over all, 43 feet on deck, 39'-3" on the l.w.l, 14 feet beam, and 6'-6" draft. The lines are very like those of the extreme Baltimore clipper schooners of the slave trade type, the only difference being in the stern. The entrance is sharp and the forefoot is slightly clubbed, or bulbous. The stem has a strong rake. The run is long and well

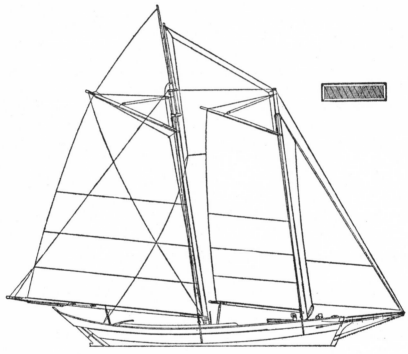

Figure 38. Sail plan of an Eastport pinky of about 1850

formed; the strong drag of the keel and the great rake of the stern-post are particularly noticeable. The long keel made these craft steady on their helm in rough going, while the raking ends made them fairly quick in stays. The body plan shows that the designer realized the importance of getting the ballast, usually broken stone and gravel, as low as possible. The hollow floors, hard bilges and flaring sides increased initial stability and power to carry sail, without making a hull that was hard to drive. The lines are capable of but slight improvement, though the buttocks might be eased a trifle. Such a vessel would be weatherly and fast in heavy going, and yet comfortable.

Like most pinkies, she had a low raised deck forward, over the forecastle and galley, which were entered through a companionway in a small trunk. The foremast was well forward and a small iron winch was located on the bowsprit bitts up in the eyes of her. Originally, she might have had a wooden windlass in place of the winch. The galley stack came through the trunk and was of iron, fitted with the common elbow. There were three hatches in the deck, as shown in the plan, the largest being the cargo hatch, or, in some boats, the hatch to the fish well. The aftermost one appears to have been used as a steering well. There was a wooden bitt and a wooden barreled pump forward of this hatch. The gammoning was a bent iron rod, driven through the head athwartships, below an iron drift-bolt in the cutwater, bent up along the sides of the bowsprit and threaded. The construction was the same as that of the old Essex pinkies, the workmanship being rough but strong. Some pinkies had but one strike in the bulwark, leaving it open at the deck and just under the rail cap. The height of the bulwarks was increased amid-ships by washboards. The "wale" or thick strakes are shown on the plans. The fastenings are of iron and locust "trunnels." The hull is ceiled from keelson to deck beams.

The rig, shown in Figure 38, requires little attention here. It is a simple schooner rig, designed for ease of handling and cheapness rather than for beauty. The boom crotch and foresail sheet cleat on the mainmast are typical fittings of the pinky. Hemp rigging was employed throughout, except for the chain bobstay. Some of these boats did not even have deadeyes, the shrouds being set up on the chain plate eyes without use of a lanyard. The old craft had rope gammoning, in the old-fashioned way. In many ways, the rig of these boats was crude, but it must be admitted that it was practical.

The possibilities of the pinky type for yacht use have not been fully investigated, but it seems evident that the pinky yacht is practical in designs whose deck lengths are between 30 and 60 feet. The hull could be utilized with other rigs, such as the sloop, cutter

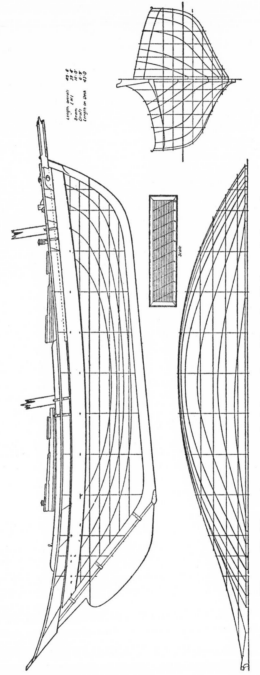

Figure 39. Lines of a proposed pinky yacht with only slight variations of the Eastport model

and ketch, but the yawl rig would be impractical. There is about as much room below in the pinky as in the common small schooner of good form. There is no question but that it would be possible to develop any cabin arrangement suitable for a schooner of the same dimensions. Full headroom is no greater a problem in the pinky than it is in the average yacht of similar size.

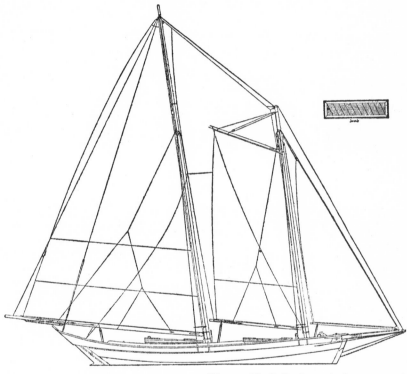

Figure 40. Sail plan of the proposed pinky yacht shown in Figure 39

Figures 39 and 40 show a slight modification of the Eastport model, fitted as a yacht. So far as the lines are concerned, the changes are few; the ends have been fined a little, to ease the buttocks, and thus, a small reduction of displacement has resulted. The appearance has altered very little. The gammon head knee was omitted, and the sheer was raised slightly forward. The lines were faired to the rabbet instead of to the face of the stem, as is modern practice. This gives an external cutwater, which is not so handsome as the faired stem of the common yacht, but is much stronger and gives much more protection to the hood-ends of the planking.

The rig is an adaptation of the modern small schooner rig with the leg-of-mutton mainsail, and is approximately of the same areas as the original example.

The design shown is capable of development, and can be modified within reasonable limits without improving" the type out of existence. It seems evident that we are under no necessity of importing foreign types and designs when we desire a seaworthy cruiser. We have a wide range of double-ender types in our own front yard, all being developed for the conditions met on our coasts and of varying size and draft. Why, then, continue to import types of doubtful value for use in our waters?

Chapter Ten

⚓

NOVA SCOTIA TERN SCHOONERS

Chapter Ten

⚓

NOVA SCOTIA TERN SCHOONERS

THE mention of a three-masted schooner, to most yachtsmen, calls to mind the common coaster, full-ended and rather clumsy. There is a type of three-master, however, that is fast and handy; one that is suitable for conversion to yachting purposes. As a matter of fact, one such schooner has already been converted to a yacht. This particular type is, usually, handsome and, in spite of the size, not extremely expensive to build or fit out.

As far back as 1800, American schooner builders had experimented with sharp, fast, three-masted schooners. These proved successful, but the end of the wars of the early nineteenth century stopped their development; with the coming of peace, speed ceased to be as important a consideration as it had been. Hence, the three-masted schooner rig, because of its advantages, became the favorite of the coasters, whose vessels were usually rather full-ended and slow, as carrying capacity was of great importance in such craft.

Since the advantages of the three-masted schooner rig have been referred to, it will not be out of place to specify them. As a sailing vessel increases in size, the problem of handling the sails becomes increasingly acute; this is particularly true in fore-and-afters. Increase in size takes form in increased length more commonly and in greater proportion than in other dimensions. As a result, there is a tendency to increase the number of masts as the length of schooners becomes great and by this means to make the individual sails smaller than would be the case if the two-masted rig were merely enlarged in proportion to the increased hull size. The smaller sails require a smaller crew to handle them, yet the total sail area necessary to drive the vessel is not sacrificed, and wear and tear on gear is not great. It may be observed that the range of length in practical three-masted schooners is between 75 and 150 feet; above these limits more masts are required. Experienced commercial schooner sailors declare that the three-master is more weatherly and handier than schooners of four or more masts.

In 1875 another attempt to develop a fast three-masted schooner began with the building, at Essex, Mass., of the *Lizzie W. Matheson,* a rather sharp three-masted "banker." She was a broad and

A TERN SCHOONER

shoal keel schooner, having a fairly sharp entrance and well-formed run; her midship section had moderate deadrise. The *Matheson* was 105 feet over all, 25'-6" beam, and 10'-5" depth of hold. She was followed by a few others of the same rig and general hull design, both in New England and in Nova Scotia, but it was considered that they were too large for the fisheries and so the experiment was not continued. Of course, individual three-masted schooners were built with speed in view, both before and after the experiment at Essex, but they were too few and scattered to constitute a type.

When the World War broke out in 1914, the demand for sailing tonnage was tremendously increased, particularly in Nova Scotia. This province had for years traded in salt fish with South America, the West Indies and the Mediterranean. It was the custom to bring

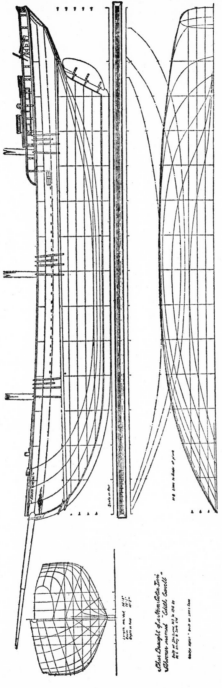

Figure 41. Lines of a Nova Scotian tern schooner, EDITH CAVELL

the salt used in curing this fish from the West Indies. In all these voyages, schooners had come into general use long before the war; many of them, though somewhat on the coaster model, were fairly fast. The war needs increased the premium on speed and the demand for schooners suitable for more than one trade. To meet the new requirements, Nova Scotian modelers turned to the modern fishing schooner for inspiration, and adapted their hull form to the three-masted rig and to the requirements of the war-time trades.

This class of modern three-masted schooner is referred to by Nova Scotiamen as the "tern schooner," a term which gives many the impression that this is the type-name of this particular class of vessel. However, this is not the case, as the Nova Scotiamen, very properly, call all three-mastered schooners by this name. Though the name for three-masted schooners is not commonly used in the United States now, it was in use in the fifties and may be seen in newspapers of that period. "Tern" means a "series of three," according to the dictionary. It may be seen, then, that the name applies not only to the fast, modern three-masters, but also to the coaster. It is with the modern class of tern schooner that this chapter will deal, however.

The lines shown in Figure 41, are those of the tern schooner *Edith Cavell,* built at Shelbourne, N. S., in 1916 by W. C. McKay & Sons, Ltd. This firm built a sister ship, the *Gladys Hollet,* at the same time. Both were owned in Newfoundland. The *Hollet* was torpedoed by a German submarine, on the coast of Nova Scotia, but was towed into Halifax and repaired, and she was still afloat in 1930. The *Cavell* was sold to Spain after the war. The *Cavell* and her sister ship were employed in the salt fish trade to the Mediterranean during the war, occasionally making a trip to Oporto. The lines of these two little schooners may be said to represent the general design of most of the vessels in this trade. The *Cavell* and the *Hollet* were round stem keel schooners, 116'-8" molded length, 26'-2" molded beam and 10'-9" depth of hold, with short quarter decks and top-gallant forecastles. The deck plan was as follows: The forecastle companionway was just forward of the foremast, there was a cargo hatch between fore and mainmasts,

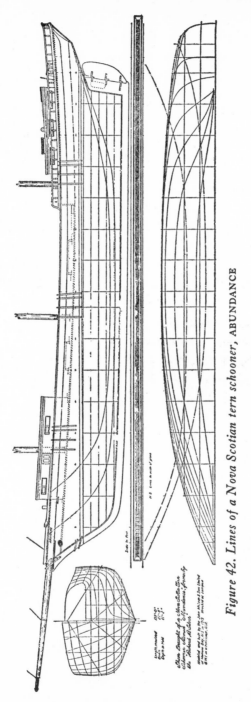

Figure 42. Lines of a Nova Scotian tern schooner, ABUNDANCE

and another just forward of the break of the quarter deck; the arrangement of the quarter deck may be seen on the plan. These two schooners were good sailers and excellent sea boats. In such small schooners as these, the run is very well formed, considering the area of the midsection necessary in such comparatively large carriers. A few vessels of somewhat similar design were built at Essex during the war.

One of the well-known builders of these tern schooners, John McLean and Sons Ltd., of Mahone Bay, N. S., designed and built the remaining three examples to be described. These were all built the same year, 1919, and represent three distinct designs. The first is the *Abundance,* formerly the *Richard B. Silver,* shown in Figure 42. She was built for Captain A. H. Zinck and others, of Lunenburg, N. S., for the Brazilian and the Mediterranean fish trade. The model used for this schooner was one made for a smaller round stern schooner; in laying this down, the bow was changed to the clipper type, and the hull lengthened and deepened. The result is shown in the lines. A fast schooner was desired; that the *Richard B. Silver* fulfilled all requirements may be seen by her passages.

Captain Zinck had the *Richard B. Silver* for nine voyages to Brazil; his longest passage was 38 days, St. Johns, Newfoundland, to Bahia, more than 4,300 miles, and his shortest was 23 days. According to the Captain, he made one run from Shelburne, N. S. to Barbados, B. W. I., 1855 miles, in 9 days, averaging nearly 8.6 knots. Captain Louis Kennedy bought the *Silver* and renamed her the *Abundance.* He made some very fast passages in this schooner, particularly in 1932 when he drove her from Halifax, N. S., to Funchal, Madeira, 2300 miles, in 14 days and 19 hours. In the same year he ran from Shelburne to Barbados in 12 days 12 hours with a full cargo. Captain Kennedy had the misfortune to lose her in a hurricane at Jamaica late in 1932. The captains who had the *Abundance* were all enthusiastic about her speed, and Captain Kennedy considered her the finest schooner in the trade. He thought that the only possible improvement would be to increase the flare forward and to lighten the counter a little. The *Abundance* was considered to be the proper size for her trade and rig. She was 138 feet molded

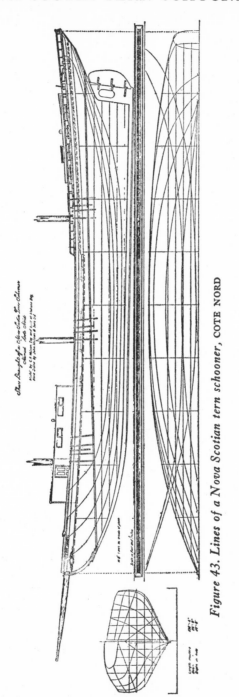

Figure 43. Lines of a Nova Scotian tern schooner, COTE NORD

length, 27'-8" molded beam and 11'-2" depth of hold, according to the information received with the model, but the sail plan indicated that another two feet had been added amidships, though this is uncertain; therefore the plan shows her as 138 feet. She was bored for a shaft, but no engine was ever installed.

Figure 43 shows the lines of another striking tern schooner, built in 1919 by the same builders, for the fur trade in Hudson Bay. This vessel is the *Cote Nord,* 136'-4" molded length, 26 feet molded beam and 10'-6" depth of hold. She was long and low, extremely easy and sharp in form, and of comparatively small displacement. In type she represents the fisherman model in the tern schooner. After being employed as a fur trader for a few years she was sold to Americans as a rum runner and became well known on Rum Row. Unlike most tern schooners, the *Cote Nord* had a bald-headed rig and was fitted with a 200 h.p. engine. As a result, her sail plan was small and this prevented her from reaching under sail the high speed possible with her hull form. Under power the *Cote Nord* was very fast. Had this vessel been given a full rig she would undoubtedly have been extremely fast under sail. The small size of her rig may be ascertained from her spar dimensions: Mizzen, quarter deck to truck, 75'-6"; main, deck to truck, 76 feet; foremast, deck to truck, 73'-6"; the bowsprit was 23'-6" outboard, including a 5'-6" pole; mizzen gaff, 35 feet; main and fore gaffs, 27'-6"; mizzen boom, 55'-6"; main and fore booms, 28 feet; and jumbo boom, 22'-6". The *Cote Nord* was suitable for conversion to a yacht and her hull was quite taking to the eye.

The lines in Figure 44 are those of the tern schooner *Marjory Mahaffy,* also built in 1919 by the McLeans, on the model of the *Mildred Adams,* lengthened 52 inches amidships. Both of these schooners had reputations for speed, and after a glance at the *Mahaffy's* plans no explanation is required. The *Mahaffy* was 130'-3" molded length, 25'-2" molded beam and 11'-3" depth of hold. The close relation of the tern schooner to the modern two-masted fisherman can be seen in this example. The *Mahaffy* and the *Adams* would compare favorably with the best crusing schooners in the yachting fleet.

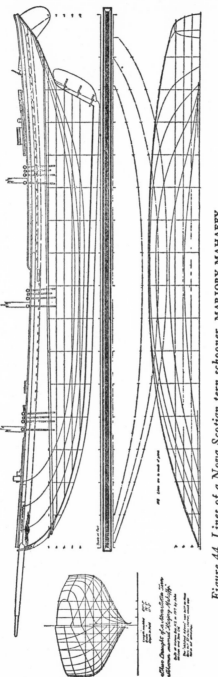

Figure 44. Lines of a Nova Scotian tern schooner, MARJORY MAHAFFY

These tern schooners were usually rather heavily rigged, and Figures 45 and 46 show the rig of the *Edith Cavell* and the *Abundance*. In general, these schooners were rigged in the same manner as a modern fisherman, except that some vessels had turnbuckles instead of deadeyes and lanyards. Some captains prefer these, as they say it is easier to set up the shrouds with the turnbuckles than with the older gear. Most of the schooners built in recent years have had spike bowsprits, though many new coasters and lumber carriers have retained the old bowsprit and jibboom. Apparently there has

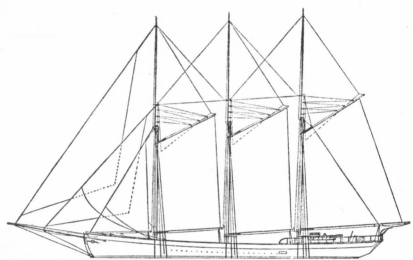

Figure 45. Sail plan of the EDITH CAVELL

been but one knockabout tern schooner built. This was the *Marne*, built at Essex about the end of the war. However, there were one or two trawler hulls fitted out as tern schooners, without bowsprits, sailing out of Gloucester after the war.

It will be noticed that the Nova Scotia tern schooner was usually of rather shoal draft in relation to her length; this is caused by the requirements of the West Indian trade, where the harbors limit the draft of vessels to about twelve feet. It is probable that an increase in the depth of the keel-shoe of most of the tern schooners of the class just described would improve their weatherliness in a breeze. In a commercial vessel, the increased draft would be objectionable, but in a yacht this would not ordinarily be true. In large schooners, such as these, the addition of outside ballast would be of doubtful value.

The construction of the schooners under discussion is that common in most large wooden vessels. The frames are sawn, double, with chocks, as is usual in fishing vessels and coasters. In Nova Scotia, birth and spruce, to a large extent, replace the oak and pine used in New England; but the soft wood Nova Scotiaman will last nearly as long as a hardwood schooner if she is well salted. With

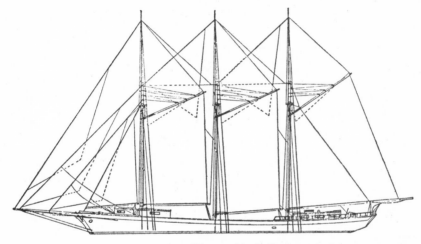

Figure 46. Sail plan of the ABUNDANCE

reasonable care, a soft wood schooner should last 17 years, as compared with 20 years, the average life of a hardwood vessel. In the Nova Scotiamen that I have inspected, the finish is of a high order and the vessels, generally, seem well fastened and strong. The only serious objection to the soft wood schooner is that the spruce planking scars easily and soon becomes unsightly, hence hardwood topside planking is often used. When employed in the West Indian salt trade and in carrying salt fish, these vessels soon become well salted from their cargoes.

Three-masted schooner yachts built in recent years have not been uniformly good sailers. Perhaps this is one of the reasons why so few are to be seen in the American yachting fleet. Another reason is the conception among many yachtsmen that the three-masted schooner must be a large vessel. A yacht designed on the Nova Scotian model would have unusually large accommodations below deck, as well as a lot of useful deck space. The question of deckhouses is a troublesome one. These are certainly convenient in a commercial schooner, to house the crew and deck machinery, but the windage of such structures is great, affecting the sailing qualities. Furthermore, deckhouses, if extended along a great proportion of the length of a vessel, as is often done in large yachts, are dangerous. This may seem a broad statement, but when we consider the difficulty of an officer seeing both sides of the deck when handling the gear, and the fact that the lee alleyways are often impassable in a heavy sea, it will be seen that long deckhouses may easily be the cause of bad accidents. Hence, if a deckhouse must be used, it should be short and narrow; in spite of the windage, the best location for such a structure seems to be forward.

Most schooner yachts of large size are flush decked; this seems to me to be a mistake. All captains of commercial schooners prefer the raised quarter deck for reasons that seem applicable to the design of large sailing yachts. These are: The better accommodations possible in the cabin with the greater useful space in the wings, due to the higher cabin floor; the better position of the helmsman in conning the ship and the dry deck for officers, owner and guests, that is possible with such construction. A sea coming aboard forward will seldom go abaft the break of the quarter deck. Except for the first, these reasons apply both to the high quarter deck of the *Abundance* and the low one of the fisherman type, as represented in the *Mahaffy*. The high quarter deck is practical only when combined with deep bulwarks. So far as hull is concerned, there are many features of the commercial schooners that could be utilized to advantage in large yachts. In rig and in spars, however, the three masted schooner yachts have followed the practice of the commercial type to a large extent. One feature common to both classes is the equal length of all three masts, or at least their regularity in comparative height. This is not particularly graceful and, in my opinion, detracts from the appearance of both hull and rig.

It would be possible to correct this rather ugly feature of the three-masted schooner rig by making foremast and mizzenmast (often called the spanker by sailors and builders) a little shorter than the main; with this arrangement of masting the foremast should be somewhat longer than the mizzen. In general, the effect would be somewhat similar to that of the old square rigged ships. The difference in the length of the masts of the schooner would not need to be so great as to cause the fore and main gaffs to foul the spring stays.

There are great possibilities in the design of yachts along the lines of the Nova Scotia tern schooner, and it is to be hoped that in our yachting fleets the type will not be neglected, as it has been in the past.

Chapter Eleven

⚓

THE BAHAMA SHARPSHOOTERS

Chapter Eleven

⚓

THE BAHAMA SHARPSHOOTERS

THE Bahama boats, as a whole, are poor craft; nevertheless, there is one type that deserves our attention. This type is found around Eleuthra Island, and is well known in the Bahamas for its speed and handiness. Eleuthra once had a great fruit-raising industry of which pineapples were the principal crop. Now this is gone, and the inhabitants engage in fishing and sponging, though a little farming is still done.

A glance at the chart will show Eleuthra to the eastward of Nassau, the capital and metropolis of the group, on New Providence Island. This island is separated from Eleuthra by the northern portion of Exuma Sound and the bight formed by the Keys to the northward, called "Cochrane Anchorage." To the southeastward of New Providence there is a great stretch of shoal and dangerous water, studded with coral "heads" and reefs. These waters are often very rough. The weather varies from flat calms to the wild West Indian hurricane, the prevailing winds being the strong easterly Trades, with occasional hard northers during the winter months. The poverty of the people on Eleuthra does not permit their employing large vessels, or power craft, hence they have had to develop a small and inexpensive, but seaworthy and weatherly sailboat.

About eighty years ago, sometime in the fifties, a Staten Island boatbuilder named Benjamin Morton became ill, as a result of which he was ordered by his doctor to take a sea voyage. As winter was coming on it was suggested that he go to the West Indies. At this period there were a number of fast schooners carrying fruit from the Bahamas and the other West Indian islands to New York, so

Morton found it cheap and convenient to take passage on one of these vessels. It happened that the schooner on which Morton took passage was bound for Tarpum Bay, Eleuthra Island, a small settlement on the western side of the island.

On Morton's arrival there he went ashore and, while the schooner was loading, he explored the island and adjacent waters. He found the climate and the planters so much to his liking that he decided to settle there. Returning to Staten Island, he sold his business and home and, with his family, came back to Tarpum Bay where he purchased land, built a house, and settled down to the life of a West Indian planter.

Living in the Bahamas without a boat is a great handicap, as Morton soon found. Carefully considering weather and water conditions, he modeled a small sailboat to suit them, and his own requirements as well. He had spent enough time in the islands to know exactly what he would need; he liked to fish in Exuma Sound, he had to have a handy ship and one that could be safely worked single-handed. The boat must be large enough, however, to carry passengers and produce to Nassau; this meant that she would have to meet possible bad weather.

Morton built, therefore, a keel catboat, rigged and modeled somewhat like the local dinghies, but larger, deeper, sharper, and more able. This boat was about 36 feet long on deck, and is said to be still afloat. She was named *Sharpshooter* and was an excellent sailer. Her good qualities were so evident that Morton's neighbors begged to buy her and finally one, a negro, was able to buy her, to the disappointment of the others. These prevailed upon Morton to build them similar boats, with the result that a new Bahama type came into being, and, because the first boat had become so well known, this type took the name "sharpshooter." Morton's practice was to build these boats, of varying sizes, on speculation, and to try them out himself to obtain the proper trim and ballasting before selling them. They ranged in length on top from 18 to 40 feet, all having the same general lines and rig. Locally, the sharpshooters are often called "sharpies," or "sharps" and are used throughout the Bahamas today.

THE BAHAMA SHARPSHOOTERS

In model, the sharpshooters, in their underbody profile, particularly, show the influence of the old Baltimore clippers, and also the influence of the local dinghies, which are like the old ship's boats. The rig of these dinghies was described in an article in *Yachting* a few years ago, written by the then commissioner at Andros Island, Mr. E. W. Forsyth, and this rig is still the most common in the islands. The sharpshooter's rig is exactly like that of the dinghy's in

A BAHAMA SHARPSHOOTER

most cases; a single loose-footed leg-of-mutton, set on a somewhat raking mast, and spread with a boom and outhaul, cutter-fashion. These sails are always fitted with a large headboard and have tremendous roach to the foot.

The hull has a good deal of deadrise and much drag to the keel. The greatest beam is a little forward of amidships, and there is usually a strong sheer. The stem is straight and raking, the transom is like that of a ship's boat, and rakes about twice as much as the stem. The mast of a sharpshooter has more rake than that of a dinghy, has no shrouds or stay, and is a heavy stick, of yellow pine.

On certain occasions a large number of sharpshooters gather at some town on Eleuthra and race to Nassau. A thrash up against a hard norther always proves popular. These boats are at their best when working to windward against a heavy sea and a strong breeze. They steer well off the wind, being an improvement on the usual centerboard catboat in this respect; they sail very fast on a reach, and show to advantage when paced by a crusing yacht of the same length and displacement. The Bahama boats are usually so run down and have such worn-out and neglected sails and gear that it is only on rare occasions that one is able to obtain a fair idea of their qualities. The only objection to the keel catboat is the difficulty of getting them out of irons without a knockdown, which, though not dangerous, is disconcerting. If a centerboard cat inadvertently gets into irons, two courses are open in order to get out; if the wind is light the helm is put over and the boat allowed to gather sternway so that she comes around on her helm. In a strong breeze, however, this is followed by a knockdown. This maneuver is what must be carried out in a keel cat. In the centerboarder, however, it is better to raise the board and let the boat swing around on her skeg, taking care to handle the mainsheet at the same time and so avoid a knockdown. Obviously, a knockdown in a well ballasted keel cat is not as potentially dangerous as in a centerboarder.

While in the Bahamas in 1924 I attempted to get a half-model of a sharpshooter, but without success, as the builders were away the day I was in Tarpum Bay. However, I did get some measurements and notes and recently a friend in the islands procured the take-off of a half-model for me, as well as very complete measurements of the sharpshooter shown in Figure 47. This boat was fairly old, and was supposed to have been built by Felix O'Neil, of Tarpum Bay. She has a somewhat sharper entrance than most sharpshooters, and was a fast boat. The Morton family still lives on Eleuthra and still builds sharpshooters, I believe, but I have not seen any recent boats built by them.

Figure 47 shows the above-mentioned sharpshooter and may be

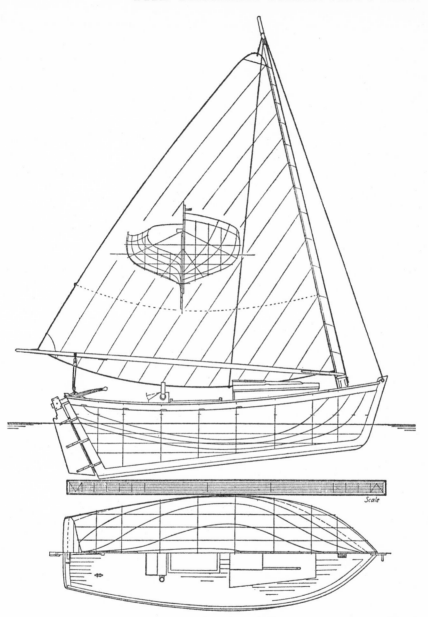

*Figure 47. A typical Bahaman sharpshooter. She is
24'-4" on deck with beam of 9 feet and draft of 4'-4"*

accepted as typical. She is a small example of the type, 24'-4" long on deck, and 9 feet beam. She draws 4'-4" when in her best trim. The proportions, as illustrated in these dimensions, seem to apply to sharpshooters of all sizes, though there is often a slight reduction of beam in the larger boats. All the Eleuthra-built sharpshooters have the planked-up deadwood, but the Nassau-built copies often have a skeg instead; it is claimed that this prevents fast sailing. The Bahama builders, when speaking of length, refer to length on the keel rather than length on top. Therefore, the length of this boat is described as being "20 feet," instead of 24'-4".

The lines show a hull with a very long run, combined with a short, hollow entrance; the greatest beam is well forward, which tends to form a somewhat marked shoulder at a point just abaft the third station from the bow. Nevertheless, the hull is well formed for speed, provided the boat is not sailed at too great an angle of heel. Usually, the hull is a well balanced one and is easy to drive. The model is seaworthy, and should be quite stiff.

The deck layout is typical of the small Bahama craft. There is a small portable trunk forward, over the forecastle, which can be unshipped to convert the forecastle into a cargo hold. There are usually no berths in the forecastle as the crew bunk on the floor, or on deck. Abaft the trunk there is either a fish well or a cargo hold, access to which is obtained by a small hatch. There is no cockpit; these craft are flush aft, which makes them uncomfortable to steer. The galley is on deck, and usually consists of a charcoal pot, a sand box, or an old-fashioned deck stove. This last is an old institution in the West Indies; it is of sheet iron and looks like a miniature piano case, with openings at each end for sheet iron stove pipe and elbow. The windward opening is usually covered by a hinged cover, there being one at each opening. Some have a hinged cover over the front as well. The pots and pans are slung from hooks and cranes located at the top of the hood, and the bottom of the stove is covered with sand and bricks. Cooking in this range is like cooking in an open fireplace. Charcoal is the popular fuel in all these galleys. The deck galley is usually placed abaft the hatch, or between the trunk and the hatch, unless the trunk is aft, as is sometimes the case in the larger boats, the galley then being placed just abaft the mast. The mast is stepped on the stem knee and is often square at the partners. It has a strong rake which brings the partners well aft. The stemhead is carried high above the bulwarks; an iron pin is driven through the stemhead athwartships and on this the halliard and the mooring cable are belayed as required. This is reminiscent of the old Essex-built Chebacco boats. All the Bahama craft, except some of the very large schooners, steer with a tiller.

The rig is extremely simple. There is but one halliard, which is belayed to the stemhead and acts as a forestay. The mainsheet is single and the deck block is mounted on a short iron horse on the transom. Some of the larger sharpshooters have a standing topping-lift. A running lift would be an improvement. A tricing line, reeving through a block aloft, is used to trice up the foot of the sail, the fall belaying to a cleat on the mast, or on deck. A single-part outhaul is employed on the mainboom. The tack is sometimes secured to the boom, but this tends to cause the boom to lift. A better plan is to secure the tack to an eyebolt on deck. In the smaller sharpshooters the sail is laced to the mast; in large boats mast-rings are used.

The advantages of the rig may be summarized as follows. A much shorter mast is possible than with the modern leg-of-mutton rig; no shrouds to be set up and watched, and, due to the rake of the mast, the center of effort does not shift so much in reefing, which makes for easier steering in heavy weather. One objection to modern leg-of-mutton rigged catboats is their lack of balance when reefed, which could be largely overcome by raking the mast as is done in the sharpshooter. Reefing, in the Bahama rig, is easily accomplished by tricing up the foot. The sail can be scandalized by letting go the tack and tricing up the sail. Of course, this does not look well, but it is certainly handy. A reef may be put in, in the usual manner, if desired, as there are generally one or more lines of reef points. If properly cut and made, the sail sets well on all points of sailing, and is efficient. The chief objection to this sail is the inability to see to leeward unless the sail is triced up. Another objection is that it is necessary to lift the foot of the sail over the top of the trunk, due to the excessive goring or roach of the foot. Both these objections can be overcome by cutting the sail higher, thus raising the rig.

The sail is made of rather heavy canvas, and the roping at the foot is heavy. The tack and the clew are strongly patched as there is a heavy strain on the lower portion of this type of sail. The head-board is made of two pieces of plank, one piece on each side of the sail, through-fastened, the roping of the sail going over the top of the headboard. The halliard is spliced into a hole bored through all. The reef cringles are also heavily patched and reinforced.

The construction of the older boats was rather good in strength and finish, but, with few exceptions, boats built during the last thirty years are very poor, and are very roughly finished. They do not compare with boats built in the States in these respects. No steam bending is to be seen in the frames; sawn frames are employed in all Bahama types, from the 13-foot dinghy to the three-masted schooner. In the dinghies and the sharpshooters the frames are of maideira, known also as "horseflesh." In small craft the frames are often single, but double frames are the most common. Some have no floors, but most do. The frames are widely spaced (18 inches on centers in the example) and are rather heavy in scantling. The construction differs little from that employed in small schooners, except in size. Planking, deck, deck beams, trunk, keel, transom, stem, mast and boom are of yellow pine, as a rule; everything is of large scantling. Sometimes the stem is of madeira, and occasionally frames are made of black mangrove. Oak is not employed as it is subject to dry rot in this climate. Fastenings are of galvanized iron, though the older and better boats were copper-fastened. White top-sides, with a seasick green trim and bottom, is the most common color scheme.

The small Bahama working craft are owned and manned by negroes, to a large extent, and while these men are good boatmen, they are not good seamen in-so-far as having any pride in the appearance of their craft is concerned. The great loss of life that occurs periodically is not due to the poor models of their boats, nor, largely, to the weather and water conditions, but to the carelessness and shiftlessness of the negro sailor. The boats are rarely painted,

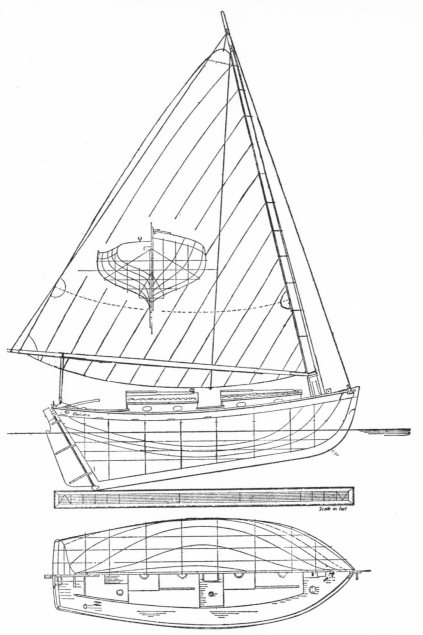

Figure 48. A proposed sharpshooter yacht. The measurements are as follows: length on deck, 24'-6"; beam, 9 feet; draft, 4'-8"

are usually leaky, and invariably have rotten gear; hence they are often in trouble. The Bahama craft were at one time a fine lot, as the early sharpshooters and turtle-schooners still afloat show, but the increasing number of colored builders and sailors has caused the various types to degenerate. The general poverty of the fishermen and spongers has necessitated their building boats as cheaply as possible, which is a contributing cause to the degeneration of the Bahama types and the numerous losses in the fishing and sponging fleets each year. To illustrate the low cost of Bahama boats, the price quoted me for building a 22-foot (keel measurement) sharpshooter, in 1924, was $250 (at Abaco). This was for the boat complete. At this price one should not expect much, but, even so, the price was ridiculously low.

In a calm, these sharpshooters can be sculled along at a good clip, once they get moving. I was told, after the hurricane of 1926, of a negro who sculled a 28-foot sharpshooter two days and one night without stopping, after his boat had become dismasted, because he was afraid that if he stopped he would not have enough strength left to get her moving again. I have seen these boats sculled "twin screw" by two men, by means of sweeps on each quarter. The boat moved at a greater speed than I could row a dinghy.

This type appears to offer possibilities as a yacht. Figure 48 is an attempt to improve upon the original type with the idea of procuring a safe and easily handled single-hander for use in exposed waters. At the same time, care was taken that the cost of building would not be unduly increased; hence outside ballast and a stern overhang were omitted. The rig was raised to overcome the objections previously noted. This made it needful, I thought, that the depth be increased slightly and the inside ballast lowered, and necessitated a slight hollow in the floors, which will make the boat a little easier to plank, as the twist in the garboards is lessened somewhat. The point of greatest beam was moved slightly aft to remove the shoulder seen in the original hull, and the rig, therefore, was moved aft and the forefoot rounded off to bring the centers into proper relationship again. I think I have improved the lines somewhat by these minor changes. The basic hull design is unchanged, however.

THE BAHAMA SHARPSHOOTERS

Some changes were made in the details of the rig in order to get the features of a single-hander. That is, all running rigging is to belay within reach of the helmsman. For this reason, the fall of the halliard and the fall of the toppinglift both reeve through a double block on the stemhead and lead aft, instead of belaying on the stemhead, as formerly. The pin through the stemhead is retained for mooring and to prevent the anchor rode from jumping out of the chock formed in the bulwarks at the bow. The tricing line is also brought aft, reeving through a deck block. The tackle likewise is brought aft; the tackle-fall reeves through a block on deck. In this manner, it will be possible to belay all important gear within reach of the helmsman. A jig on the outhaul may enable a man to set up the mainsail better, so this has been added.

A small self-bailing cockpit seems desirable, and in a boat lacking a headroom it is best that it should not be necessary to move about any marked distance in the cabin. Therefore, the double house has been employed.

The arrangement proposed gives two berths and a W. C. in the forward cabin; stove, sink and ice box in the after cabin just abaft the bridge deck, with seats, table and clothes locker also, in the after trunk. Under the bridge deck will be located the tanks for fresh water, part of the ice box, and a coal or wood locker. The trunks are to be lighted by two deck lights of the prism type in each, as well as by the usual cabin ports. A pin rack under the tiller will act as a tiller comb, and enable the tiller to be fixed in any desired position. Inside ballast will be broken sash weights.

The advantage of the sharpshooter is that she is a safe type of catboat and possesses many of the good qualities of the cat, as well as some of her own.

Chapter Twelve

⚓

BERMUDA SLOOPS AND DINGHIES

BERMUDA SLOOPS AND DINGHIES

IN THE early part of the seventeenth century the shipbuilders of Jamaica developed an interesting type of sloop. During the whole of the seventeenth and most of the eighteenth centuries the Caribbean Sea was a hotbed of piracy and warfare. Buccaneers, pirates, privateers and naval cruisers of many nationalities cruised among the West Indian Islands, or along the coast of the mainland, and no vessel was safe from capture. As a result fast sailing craft were in great demand; to meet the existing conditions the "Jamaica sloop" was developed and soon became very popular.

Bermuda rose in importance as a shipbuilding community soon after being colonized. Having a local timber, a species of red cedar, excellent for shipbuilding purposes, the Bermudians soon became shipbuilders for all the British West Indies. By 1700 they had taken over the Jamaica sloop and had made improvements in the original model. Jamaica soon lost its importance as a shipbuilding center and within a few years the type formerly known as the "Jamaica sloop" was called the "Bermuda sloop."

Because of the speed of these sloops, the British Navy bought them for small cruisers, and the traders, privateers and pirates procured them whenever possible. Not only were the Bermuda sloops well thought of in the West Indies, but they soon had a great reputation in Europe—so great, in fact, that the famous Swedish naval architect, Chapman, thought it necessary to include the lines of a 'Mudian in his monumental work *Architecturia Mercatoria Navalis,* published 1763. The type was also well known in North

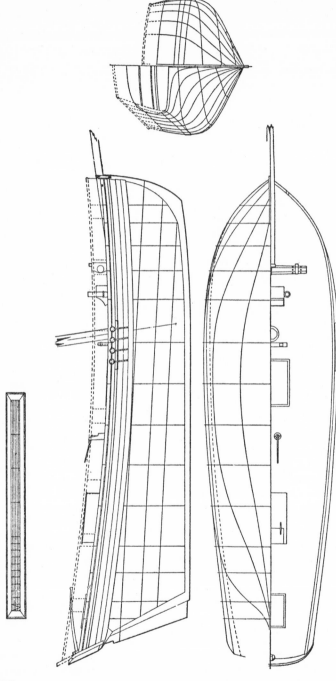

Figure 49. The lines of the sloop LADY HAMOND *as taken off in 1804. She was 68 feet over all, with beam of 20 feet. Dotted lines show alterations made for naval service*

America, and there is some indication that the Baltimore clipper schooner was a development of these sloops.

From the time of the American Revolution to about 1800, schooners gained in popularity, while large sloops lost ground. However, the Bermudians continued to be built for another forty

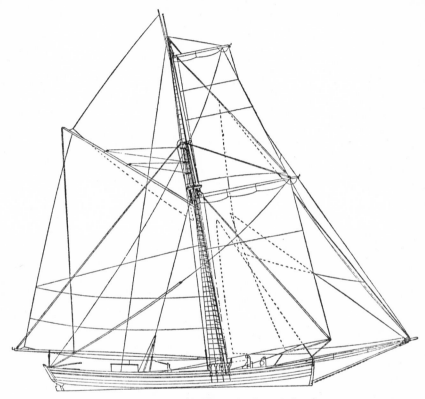

Figure 50. The sail plan of the sloop LADY HAMOND

years. These sloops differed little in rig from the contemporary New England boats except in having a more raking mast. Their hulls were broad and deep, there was much drag to the keel and quite a bit of rake to the stem and sternposts. Sometimes they were of large size; a length of 75 feet on deck was not uncommon as early as 1750. The early models had high bulwarks and raised quarter decks; later vessels were flush-decked and were usually without bulwarks other than the common log rail.

To illustrate a typical Bermudian sloop of large size, Figure 49 shows the lines of the *Lady Hamond* as taken off for the British Admiralty in 1804. At this time the Royal Navy was in need of small and fast cruisers, and purchased certain fast vessels to be used as models. First they bought a small Bermudian schooner named the *Haddock* and built some thirty copies. These proved too small, so they procured the sloop *Lady Hamond,* added bulwarks, and built a dozen copies. To these they gave rather "pretty" names, as follows: *Alphea, Alban, Adonis, Bacchus, Barbara, Cassandra, Claudia, Laura, Olympia, Sylvia, Vesta* and *Zenobia.* These (as were fifteen of the *Haddock* class) were built at Bermuda by the Messrs. Goodriche of St. Georges. The sloops were quite successful, though rather small for the purpose. One or two were rerigged as schooners, but the majority remained sloop-rigged throughout their whole existence. Some of the class went to European stations. The *Alphea,* for example, is noted as having blown up in action with a French privateer on the coast of France, another appeared in the East Indies, and the Laura was captured by an American privateer in the War of 1812. The *Lady Hamond* is an interesting design, showing that even at that early date, the advantages of a slightly rockered keel and raking sternpost, as well as of rising floors, high and hard bilges, and long run, were well known.

Figure 50 shows the sail plan of the *Lady Hamond,* drawn from the spar dimensions. The rig is that of the ordinary large sloop of the time, differing from that of the contemporary English cutter in having the mast a little farther forward and in having a fixed bowsprit instead of a reefing one.

The next class built in Bermuda, for the Royal Navy, was made up of five three-masted schooners, about 80 feet long on deck. These were built on the lines of a Baltimore-built schooner named the *Flying Fish,* a beautifully modeled three-master. These schooners turned out to be the fastest vessels in the Royal Navy and the Bermudians were so taken with them that they adopted the model as a local type. The leg-of-mutton sail had been used on two-masted small boats at Bermuda since colonial days, so it was natural that the new schooners should be given the same rig. Up until the 1830's, the three-masters were the popular type in Bermudian waters. The old sloops slowly disappeared, many of them being sold to the Brazilian slavers. As late as 1840, the old Bermudian topsail sloops are mentioned as being slavers.

With the passing years the timber on the islands had been pretty well cut off and the demand for Bermudian-built large craft had ceased, due to the competition of the Baltimore and New England builders. In the 1830's only small schooners and a few small sloops were in existence at Bermuda; the officers of the British garrison and naval officers on the station amused themselves by racing the small three-masted schooners. There is a legend to the effecct that one officer, the Honorable H. G. Hunt, having lost a schooner race, came to the conclusion that a leg-of-mutton-rigged sloop would beat the schooners to windward. The conditions of weather and water at Bermuda had much effect on racing, as the steady winds permitted the use of large rigs and the many narrow channels between the islands put a premium on windward ability. The ability to shoot a long way in stays was another desirable quality. According to the story, Hunt built the sloop and tried her out against a schooner at midnight before challenging the schooner that had beaten him. Being successful in both races, he drew the attention of his brother sailors to the possibilities of this type of sloop. As a result the schooners were all replaced by the leg-of-mutton-rigged sloops. I have not been able to learn the date of this incident and cannot vouch for the truth of the yarn. It is apparent that it must have occurred either in the late 20's or early 30's, if true. At any rate, the leg-of-mutton-rigged sloop comes into prominence during the 30's. From then on, one finds many references to the type.

As the new type developed it received much attention, due to the fact that British officers took their boats home to England. Some of these were raced against English yachts and won with ease. Not only small sloops, but also quite a number of dinghies, were taken to England. The dimensions of a typical Bermudian sloop of the 30's are those of the celebrated *Lady Ussher,* wrecked in the hurricane of 1839. Length over all, 32 feet; length on the keel, 24 feet; breadth of beam, 12 feet; draft of water, 8 feet; length of mast, 64 feet; hoist of mainsail, 56 feet. It must be observed that the draft and length of mast are those for racing. Sloops such as the *Lady Ussher* had much outside deadwood and keel, and a deep shoe was added when racing.

From the 30's to the 80's, the Bermudian sloops, with their towering rigs, were popular in the islands and were well known in England, though less well known in the United States. Apparently, a type so close to home was not considered worthy of attention by American yachtsmen. As a result, the good qualities of the leg-of-mutton and overlapping jib were not studied until very recent years.

The models of these sloops varied but little as to lines. Figure 51 shows the lines of a typical Bermudian sloop, taken off by an Englishman, a Mr. Wm. Prattent, about 1870. This gentleman was also the draftsman who drew the lines of another Bermudian, the *Diamond,* shown in Dixon Kemp's *Manual of Yacht and Boat Sailing,* 4th edition, London, 1884, and also in other editions of the same work. The only appreciable difference between the boat shown in Figure 51 and the *Diamond* is in dimensions and in the shape of the stem; the *Diamond* had a clipper bow. The *Diamond* had a little less sheer and measured 39'-6" over all, 34 feet on the water line, 11'-2½" beam, 5'-10" draft, and 6'-6" when racing. Her racing mast was about 6 feet longer than her working mast, the halliard for the racing mainsail being at the masthead. The example is apparently a working boat and is a few inches wider than the *Diamond,* as well as a little shorter and deeper. Her length over all is 37'-4", 11'-6" beam, 6'-3" draft. The dimensions of another contemporary are those of the *Julia,* 20'-9" over all, 8 feet beam, and 5 feet draft. The dimensions of still another are those of the *Undine,* pictures of which were published in *Yachting* (July, 1927). Length over all, 23'-10"; length on the water line, 21'-7½"; beam, 8'-2½"; depth of hull, 4'-6"; draft, 4'-6"; hoist of mainsail, 43'-6". *Undine* and *Julia* had clipper bows, but it is said that *Undine* had a straight stem when new; her stem rabbet was straight, whereas that of *Julia* was curved and flared outward.

The lines in Figure 51 show a fast sailing hull of moderate power. Photos of *Undine* show a very similar hull form. There

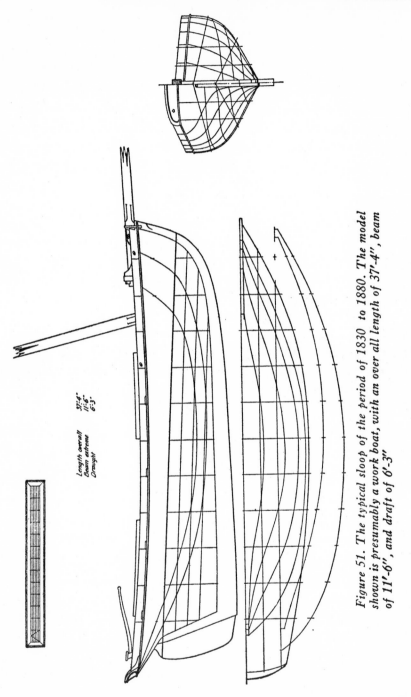

Figure 51. The typical sloop of the period of 1830 to 1880. The model shown is presumably a work boat, with an over all length of 37′-4″, beam of 11′-6″, and draft of 6′-3″

Length overall 37′-4″
Beam extreme 11′-6″
Draught 6′-3″

was no hollow in the garboards amidships and only moderate hollow in the entrance. The construction was said, by contemporary writers, to have been rather rough, and the finish of the hull poor. The frames were double, sawn, and closely spaced. The scantlings were large, but due to the lightness of the Bermuda cedar the hull was light and a large proportion of ballast to displacement was

Bermuda Sloop
Taken off about 1870, Wm Pratten
Redrawn 1931, Chapelle

Figure 52. The sail plan of the sloop shown in Figure 51

carried. The ballast was wholly inside and was composed of lead or iron pigs. When racing, some ballast was shifting. The deck arrangement depended upon the size of the boat, the larger sloops had a trunk forward, sometimes removable. The smaller boats merely had two hatches, one of which served as a cockpit. There were no bulkheads and the sloops sometimes swamped when racing. Fastenings were always of copper.

BERMUDA SLOOPS AND DINGHIES

Figure 52 is the sail plan and shows the typical rig of the Bermudians. The mainsail was loose-footed, and when racing was laced to the mast; some boats employed a headboard, while others had short yards or gaffs. An outhaul was not used to flatten the mainsail; rather, the main boom was really a sprit and was handled in the same manner as the sprits of the New Haven sharpies. A guntackle purchase at the fore end of the boom supported it and acted as the outhaul. The jib was set on a stay in the larger sloops, but on the small boats it was set flying. The jib-topsail was similarly set, to a jibboom. The jib always had some overlap and both jib and jib-topsail sheets led through the rail. When the racing mast was shipped it was usual to set up a shroud on each side, but no shrouds were considered necessary with the working rig. One of the most interesting things about this rig, however, is the peculiar topsail which was set when going free in fine weather. The topsail was simple and easily set; it is curious that no one has employed this sail on a modern jib-header. The spars were of imported white spruce.

To show the opinion prevalent among English yachtsmen as to the qualities of the rig, it will be instructive to quote H. C. Folkard's book *The Sailing Boat,* third edition, London, 1863. On page 278 the author says: "The Bermudian rig ought not to be extended to vessels above eighteen tons, because any mast fit to carry a proportionate area of canvas would be too ponderous for its position. It is unquestionably a superior mode of rig, and if not one of the fastest in the world, is considered as unequalled for working to windward in the smooth water; but in a sea way the lofty peak is not so effective. These boats are said to sail nearer the wind than cutters; this, and the quickness with which they tack, would seem to make up for any deficiency of speed on the bowline." This opinion was little different from that often expressed as to the desirability of modern jib-headers.

At the same time that the sloops were being developed a small boat was becoming popular. The importance of the small boats was greatly enhanced in the year 1840 by the victory of the *Alarm,* 13 feet long, over a celebrated sloop 25 feet long. In a light breeze, the *Alarm* worked three miles to windward in 36 minutes. These small boats were a development of the ordinary ship's boat, wholly open and fitted with a deep false keel or shoe. So popular did these boats become that a racing rule was formulated which put a limit on the size of their hulls. The small boats were known as dinghies and continued in use long after the sloops ceased to be built. The competition among the dinghies was keen and quite a number were designed in England. Dinghies were taken to England and carefully studied. For years these boats were believed to be the

BERMUDA DINGHIES

fastest small boat possible and it was not until Larry Huntington designed the half-rater *Paprika,* which was taken to Bermuda and which cleaned up the dinghies in short order, that this was questioned.

Figure 53 shows a typical Bermudian dinghy, except for a more cutaway bow than is usual. This boat was built in Bermuda, in 1887, for a Captain Fitzgerald. There is no information as to who designed her; apparently, this was done in England. The lines show a rather shapely hull, which plainly was influenced by the ship's boat. The frames were sawn and the construction was similar to that of the present Bahama dinghies. Like the sloops, the

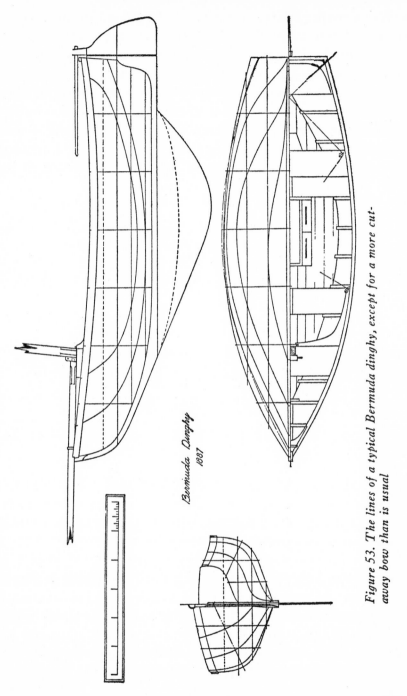

Bermuda Dinghy
1887

Figure 53. The lines of a typical Bermuda dinghy, except for a more cut-away bow than is usual

dinghies were built wholly of cedar and their topsides were like-wise oiled and varnished. The underbodies of both types were copper painted. The most remarkable feature of the dinghies was the keel. Originally of wood, it developed into a veritable fin made of iron plate. Most dinghies had two removable keels, one for racing, of iron, and a smaller one of iron or wood for ordinary sailing. Sometimes the racing fin took the form shown in the plan, while in others it was merely a rectangle. The early dinghies had longer

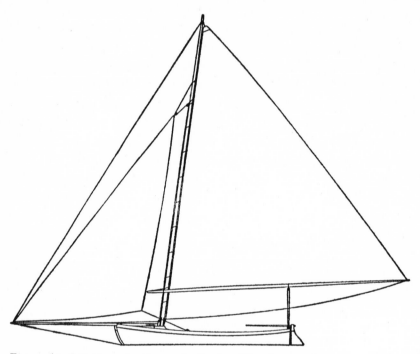

Figure 54. Sail plan of a Bermuda dinghy. The rig was always the same, though there were slight variations in proportion

and shoaler wooden shoes, much curved in profile. Ballast was lead and was shifted to windward when racing. Four men consti-tuted the racing crew. The favorite course was the "Old Bermuda Course," six miles to windward and a three-mile run.

Figure 54 gives the sail plan of the dinghy shown in the lines. The rig was always the same, though there were slight variations in proportion. A racing dinghy carried from 375 to 390 square feet of sail in mainsail and jib combined, and about 180 square feet in a spinnaker, on a hull 14 feet over all and 4'-8" in beam. In amount of sail carried in proportion to size, the Bermudian dinghies were surpassed by some of the Australian boats only. Except in their size, the rig of the dinghies offers no unusual features. The mainsail is similar to that of the sloops; the jib is set flying with single part halliards. From photos, it is judged that the jib stood well. The mainsail was laced to the mast and could not be reefed.

Both types are practically extinct today. The Bermuda cedar has totally disappeared and lumber has to be imported into the islands. As a result, boat building died out some years ago. Local boats and yachts are now imported from America and England and a visit to Bermuda in search of the old types is useless. It is a pity that the old Bermuda boats have not been retained as they would make fine yachts if slightly altered and modernized.

Chapter Thirteen

⚓

AMERICAN PILOT BOATS : I

Chapter Thirteen

⚓

AMERICAN PILOT BOATS: I

Taking all types of commercial schooners into consideration, the pilot boat most closely approaches the yacht in her requirements, since she carries no cargo and has to be fast and seaworthy. The reputations of individual schooners of the pilot boat class have been of the highest, not only for speed and weatherliness but also for beauty.

It is rather difficult to classify the variations of the pilot boat, since schooners built in one locality were often employed in another. This resulted in numerous modifications in design; to catalogue these would require more space than is available in this short study. For that reason, it is necessary to divide the general class into types, according to locality, and to treat each during the zenith of its evolution rather than to attempt to show the development of the whole class from its inception to recent times.

As far as I can judge, the pilot boats as a class were all direct descendants of a model of schooner developed on the Chesapeake some time before 1745. Just how early a date can be placed on the employment of a special model of boat in the pilot service on the Bay, or at other ports, I cannot say; at any rate, it was prior to the Revolution. Though descending from a common type, by 1812 the New York boats were a distinct model when compared with their contemporaries on the Chesapeake, while after 1850 the Boston boats differed from both. Unquestionably, this distinction of form was due to a difference in the requirements of local service; not in the customs of the pilots so much as in the weather and sea conditions to be met off each port. Nevertheless, such classification is, like the dates given, no more than a generalization, since Maryland- and Virginia-built pilot boats were used off Sandy Hook as late as the '40's, and Boston-built schooners later. It can be seen, therefore, that the distinctions made between the various models, taking them by locality and date, must often be somewhat vague.

Considering the material available as evidence, it seems possible to establish the fact that the Virginia model (this term includes

A VIRGINIA PILOT BOAT OF 1806

Maryland-built boats) was the oldest and that it was the forerunner of all other types of pilot boat along our coasts. This is sufficient reason for choosing the Virginia model as our first subject in studying the type. In addition, it is particularly expedient to do so, since the Southern boats reached a climax in development at an earlier date than the boats of the Northern ports and also went out of existence while the others were still developing.

Though advertisements, offering for sale schooners of the pilot boat model, can be found in Maryland papers dated before the

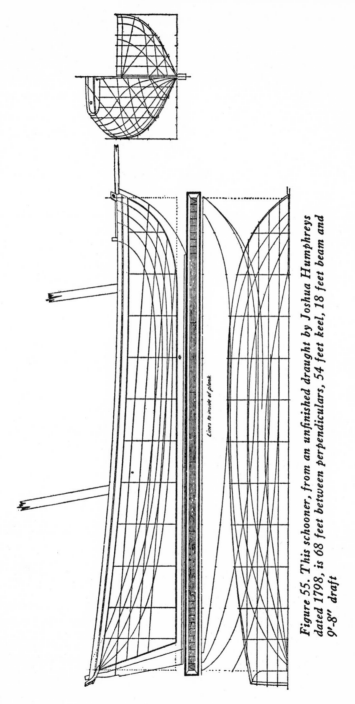

Lines to inside of plank

Figure 55. This schooner, from an unfinished draught by Joshua Humphreys dated 1798, is 68 feet between perpendiculars, 54 feet keel, 18 feet beam and 9'-8" draft

Revolution, no plans so early in date have yet come to light. In fact, it is not until the last decade of the eighteenth century that any evidence of this nature appears. Before presenting such evidence, let us try to picture the requirements of the pilot service off the Virginia Capes.

Though there was deep water off, and in, the entrance to the Bay, the havens in which a pilot boat might find shelter in bad weather were comparatively shoal. Most of the schooners used in the service were, therefore, rather shallow. However, their stations when on duty were at sea, hence seaworthiness was essential. When the pilots had boarded incoming ships, only one hand was left on the pilot boat to bring her home; consequently, the boat had to work easily. However, the boat had to be large enough to be seaworthy when loaded with the provisions needed for a stay at sea until all the pilots found ships; it was found that a schooner about 60 feet on deck was the best size to meet this requirement. In addition to these physical considerations, the popular model of pilot boat would be influenced by the prevailing ideas of the locality as to what element of design should be used as a basis of comparison of individuals. In the locality in question, speed under sail was looked upon as such a means of valuation. Of course, the pilot service being competitive, this feature took on additional importance. All these considerations combined to produce a most interesting model of schooner; the economic conditions of the service probably prevented the type from reaching undesirable extremes.

Bginning with 1798, the earliest plan whose date can be given with certainty is the one shown in Figure 55. This was an unfinished draught by Joshua Humphreys, the famous designer of the frigate *Constitution*. The original was complete except for deadwood, transom and the position of the masts. Dated 1798, this plan was probably a project for a dispatch vessel or revenue cutter; apparently it was not used. In spite of this it may be used as an example of the Virginia pilot boat, for it is obviously based on this model, judging by contemporary pictures. However, it is undoubtedly a little larger than the usual run of pilot boats. For comparison, the dimensions of a "Virginia Pilot schooner" of about the same period

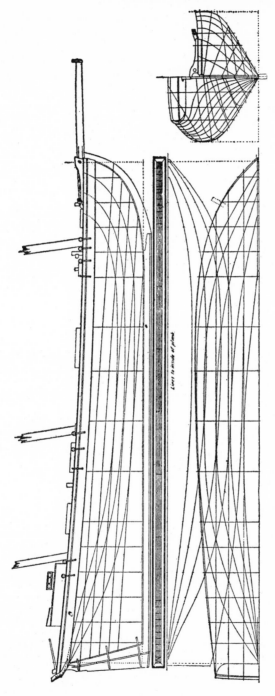

Figure 56. Another schooner from the Humphreys collection. A note says: "This vessel should have more waist. 1800."

Lines to inside of plank

were recorded as: length on the range of deck, 56 feet; length of keel for tonnage, 42'-9"; beam, extreme, 15'-3", molded, 15 feet; draft, 6'-8"; and tonnage, 53 tons. Comparison of these dimensions with those on the plan under discussion show some similarity in proportions. The Humphreys schooner is very easy-lined fore and aft and would have been a fast vessel. She shows the common features of the type, the raking ends, deep drag and low freeboard. The low "waist" or bulwarks were typical, as will be seen as we go along. In 1812, a very famous Baltimore privateer schooner, the *Rossie,* suffered heavy losses in action due to the lack of bulwarks, according to her commander, so it can be seen that even large schooners were so built.

The features of the Virginia pilot boats were used in some extreme examples of larger schooners of the "Baltimore clipper" type, as can be proven, not only by referenc to the *Rossie* but by contemporary plans. Such a plan is presented in Figure 56, which is another draught found in the Humphreys collection. It is impossible to say whether or not this schooner is a Humphreys design, though the note, in reference to the waist being too low, seems to be in Humphrey's handwriting. This plan was complete to top of waist, but the deck arrangement, number and position of the masts and chain plates are not given on the original. I have attempted to reconstruct her appearance, to some extent, assuming her to have been a three-masted schooner. My reasons for this assumption are that three-masters were rather popular at this date, and the proportions of the hull, 80 feet between perpendiculars, 65 feet on the keel, 21 feet molded beam and 8'-9" depth of hold. This schooner is somewhat lacking in stability. Now, I have another plan of a Baltimore-built schooner of approximately the same date and proportions, taken off in England in 1806, which is a three-masted schooner in rig. This is the *Flying Fish.* Like Figure 56 she had the log rail; her hull dimensions were: length on deck, 78'-8", length on keel, 60'-8", breadth, extreme, 21'-7", and depth in hold, 7'-10". Because of the rather marked similarity of dimensions and model, I think my assumption is a safe one; at any rate, I used the deck arrangement, proportional location of masts and number and location of chain-plates shown in the plan of the *Flying Fish*. If Figure 56 was a two-master, her mainmast would be placed about 8 feet farther aft than indicated in the figure. The influence of the pilot boat, in this schooner, is noticeable, as it is in the case of the *Flying Fish,* not only in hull, but in rig, in the last case. The spar dimensions of the *Fish* have recently turned up. The sails she carried were fore staysail, jib and jib topsail, fore course, fore topsail and fore topgallant, and gaff foresail. The last was without boom and overlapped the main. On the mainmast she set main course, main square topsail, and main topmast staysail or "fisherman" (set flying) ; a gaff mainsail like the fore, and a gaff topsail, set on a miniature gaff. The gaff mainsail was without a boom and overlapped. On the "driver" or mizzen, she had a boomed spanker and gaff topsail. She was fitted for stu'nsails on fore and main yards, and on fore and main topsail yards, with a ringtail on the spanker. The rig was marked by extreme simplicity, considering the number and variety of sails carried.

Strictly speaking, the schooners we have been discussing are somewhat off the subject of this chapter; nevertheless, they are so interesting and striking in appearance that no excuse appears necessary for having introduced them. It may be said that the three-masters were an intermediate step from pilot boat to the usual Baltimore clipper. Such hulls as have just been referred to are somewhat deeper in proportion to beam and length than the Virginia pilot boats, and such hulls, tow-masted, were the basis of the model of the Northern pilot boats.

A more typical Virginia pilot boat can be seen in Figures 57 and 58. The model and rig shown in these plans represent the boats as they were from 1806 to 1840 or later. The step from the early examples is slight so it appears that the developments prior to 1800 had resulted in a very satisfactory class, considering the requirements of the local pilotage. The shallowness of the hull is marked, but Marestier, the French naval constructor, who obtained this plan in 1821, remarked that she appeared somewhat lighter in draft than many of her class. In spite of the great beam and large area of midsection, the hull is well formed for speed; this is particularly

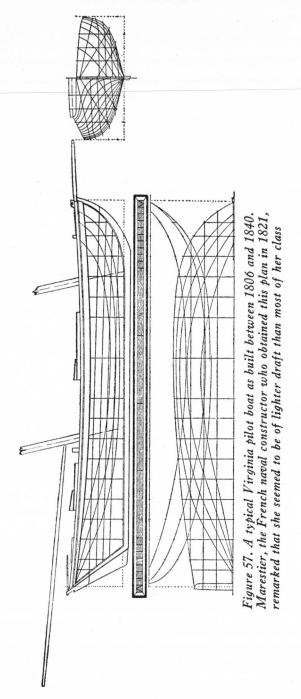

Figure 57. A typical Virginia pilot boat as built between 1806 and 1840. Marestier, the French naval constructor who obtained this plan in 1821, remarked that she seemed to be of lighter draft than most of her class

true aft. The extraordinarily thin quarters, so often apparent on these old schooners, may still be seen on the Bay. This example of the type shows the utter simplicity of the model, not only in the fitting of the hull but also in rig. There was neither winch nor capstan on deck. Beginning at the bow, we find the samson post at the heel of the bowsprit, next the foremast, then, in some boats, a galley

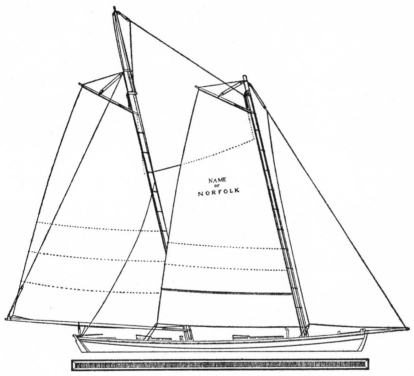

Figure 58. Sail plan of the schooner shown in Figure 57

hatch and chimney, and next, the main hatch. In pictures of these schooners, both this and the after hatch appear open. This was apparently the practice in summer, but in winter, a cover with a companionway was added to each hatch. Moving on aft, we find the mainmast and two wooden pumps, then a large after hatch, mentioned above. At the extreme stern, we discover the "standing room" or helmsman's cockpit. As one studies this boat, one is impressed by the expanse of deck space available, as well as by the low freeboard and lack of bulwarks. The knightheads are prominent in all Bay craft, even in the small sailing boats seen there nowadays.

The rig is worthy of special attention, not only for its simplicity, but also for its efficiency and low cost. In spite of the fact that this schooner is large (58 feet over all and 18′-6″ extreme beam) when compared to modern small schooners, as well as being a very stiff model, there is no standing rigging, either stays or shrouds, to be seen. As can be observed, the sail area is far from small. To make this rig stand, the mast diameters were large. 15 inches for the foremast and 14½ inches for the main. The sticks were usually of hard pine. The large jib and main topmast staysail were always set flying, thus avoiding the use of stays. The running rigging was as simple as possible, and these features, combined with low freeboard, reduced windage to a minimum. Unlike modern schooner yachts, the pilot boat could get the fullest advantage of her foresail by having it loose-footed and overlapping the mainmast. In small schooners, where foresails are often so small in area as to be of little value, the large foresail of the early schooners would be of grat value. It has been held that such a rig is awkward when in stays, as the sheet blocks are tossed about to the detriment of any heads that happen to be near. This objection can be overcome, of course, and, strangely enough, we never hear much about it in the modern cruising cutter, with her large and often overlapping fore staysail. The point is that, if overlapping headsails are to be permitted in one-masted racing yachts, to say nothing of "trick" light sails, the logic of denying the schooners the advantages of their masting obtained by the so-called "lug foresail" of the example, is hard to understand.

Returning to our mutton, other advantages of the rig shown in Figure 58 can be discovered. Because of the distribution of sail brought about by the use of so large a foresail, the pilot schooner could work and stay under the foresail alone. Ordinarily they worked under fore and mainsail only; in moderate airs the jib and maintopmast staysail were available. To furl or reef either jib or mainsail, it was not necessary to leave the deck, since the jib, being set flying, could be brought on deck by letting go both halliards and

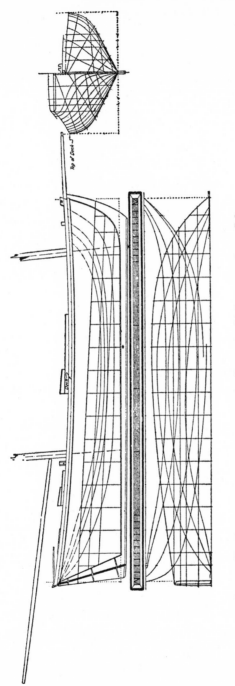

Figure 50. The schooner LAFAYETTE, the lines of which were taken off by Francis Grice, U.S.N. He says of her: "This schooner is the fastest in her business. She is without shrouds or stays."

tack. The mainsail, being loose-footed, could be brought inboard by releasing the outhaul, the traveler on the boom preventing the clew from going adrift. The large bonnet on the foresail, when unlaced, did away with an awkward roll of canvas that would otherwise result from reefing the sail and be doubly unhandy when wet. Since there were neither stays nor shrouds to bother with, changing the rake of the masts to obtain a good balance was easily accomplished.

Though the example we have just been looking at was built somewhere between 1815 and 1820, she will represent the Virginia model until the class disappears. Changes made later were of minor nature, such as less rake to the ends, more deadrise and greater or less beam and depth, within narrow limits. Figure 59 is a plan of a later and highly praised schooner of this type, the Norfolk pilot boat *Lafayette*. Her lines were taken off by Francis Grice, an able designer in the United States Navy who turned out the brig *Perry* in the '40's, considered the fastest vessel of her date in the service. Grice took off the lines of the *Lafayette* some time in 1837. She was then but a few years old though I have not yet found the date of her build. However, the reason that Grice was interested in her was that she had the reputation of being about the fastest thing of her inches around the Virginia Capes.

The Virginia pilot boat, as a type, has been out of existence for many years. With the rise of New York to supremacy as a port of entry for foreign trade, the traffic into the Chesapeake Bay became largely coasting vessels that required no pilots. As a result, the number of pilot schooners necessary for the business gradually decreased until, by 1860, but few were left. The Civil War gave the foreign and coastwise trade of the Bay such a blow that it was many years before it recovered. The disappearance of the old model of Virginia pilot boat was due, as can be seen, to a change in trade lanes rather than to faults of the type.

Chapter Fourteen

⚓

AMERICAN PILOT BOATS : II

Chapter Fourteen

⚓

AMERICAN PILOT BOATS: II

IT IS COMMONLY supposed that New York's bid for nautical fame during the days of sailing ships rests on her grand packets and swift clipper ships. Impressed though one must be by the splendor of the packets and the size, beauty and speed of the lovely—though short lived — clipper ships, it was the clean lined pilot schooners that brought recognition at home and abroad to the shipbuilders of New York, New Jersey and Long Island.

Long before the days of the packets and clipper ships, and long before the yacht *America,* that remarkable development of the pilot schooner, attracted popular attention, the pilot boats used off Sandy Hook were known to naval architects in England and on the Continent as remarkably fast, seaworthy and handsome vessels. Time and again foreign designers attempted to duplicate in their own craft the good qualities of these slippery schooners — but usually with little success.

A direct descendent of the famous Baltimore clippers, by way of the "Virginia model" of schooner, the Sandy Hook pilot schooners gradually developed certain characteristics of their own, due to the requirements of their service and the natural evolution of ideas on the part of their builders. For the greater part of their existence as a type, the Sandy Hook pilot schooners exhibited the basic principles of design employed in the old Baltimore "heelers." The modifications came into use gradually, though eventually the changes became so extensive and far-reaching that little of the older type could be distinguished. However, revivals of the old and tried models occurred right up to the end of the existence of the type,

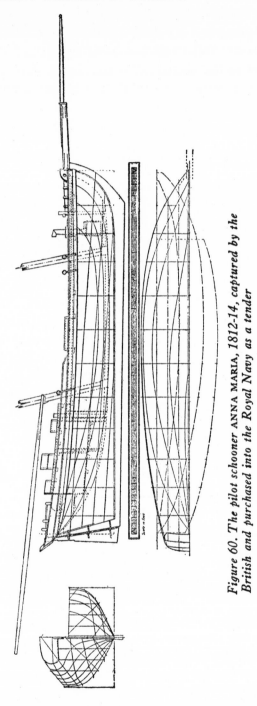

Figure 60. The pilot schooner ANNA MARIA, 1812-14, captured by the British and purchased into the Royal Navy as a tender

whenever pilots became tired of experimenting with new models.

Before attempting to trace the evolution of the Sandy Hook pilot schooners, it will be well to give a hasty picture of the conditions and requirements of the service in which these boats were employed. The entrance to New York Harbor was much more difficult in

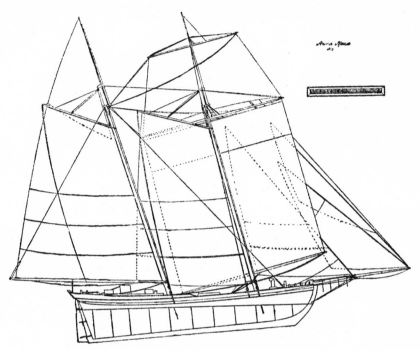

Figure 61. Sail plan of the ANNA MARIA

the old days than it is now; until comparatively recent times the channels were so poorly marked and shifted so much with each gale that local knowledge was necessary even in comparatively small vessels seeking the port. Due to the fierce competition among the pilot companies, brought about by their numbers (which, in turn, was the result of the steadily increasing commerce of the port), the schooners were forced to work well out at sea, far from shelter. Except within the harbor itself, the only shelter available to pilot boats caught inshore was the New Jersey shore close to the Hook.

The weather off the Hook leaves much to be desired in the winter and the tail-end of a West Indian hurricane sometimes makes things interesting in summer or fall. With the whole sweep of the Atlantic to windward, it is natural that a pilot schooner would have to prove her seaworthiness in such gales.

The boats were owned by companies or groups of pilots, though occasionally one might be owned by an individual. In early days, anyone so desiring could call himself a pilot — with easily imagined results. Then followed many attempts to limit and supervise the pilots, as well as to establish requirements for their training. It is not my purpose to give an account of the difficulties of the pilots in obtaining a satisfactory method of controlling and safeguarding their business nor of the abuses with which they had to contend. There is an excellent picture of this feature in *From Sandy Hook to 62°* by Charles E. Russell (The Century Co., 1929). Suffice it to say, conditions were such that there was the keenest competition, not only between the pilots themselves, but between the pilot companies of New York and New Jersey as well. This put an unusually high premium on speed in their schooners.

The greater part of the development of the Sandy Hook pilot schooner, as a type, may be said to have taken place between 1800 and 1860; the rise of the pilot boat kept pace with the increasing importance of New York as a port. The boats used after the Revolution and until 1800 seem to have been similar to the early "Virginia model" in nearly every respect. However, between 1800 and 1812 there was a gradual change in design, in the direction of greater depth and seaworthiness. This was brought about, perhaps, by the pilots going farther to sea as a result of growing competition.

By 1812, then, the Sandy Hook pilot schooners may be said to have become a particular type, and the *Anna Maria,* whose plans are shown in Figures 60 and 61, represents the popular model of that period. She seems to be a good example of her class in design, rig and dimensions. She also illustrates the fact that the "New York model" of pilot boat was known abroad at this early date, for this schooner was taken into the Royal Navy as a tender, a service requiring great speed. It was during this period, also, that the deck

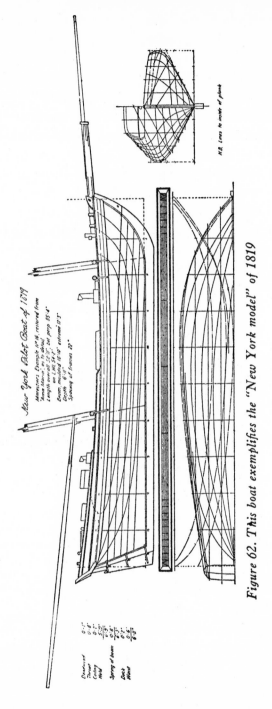

Figure 62. *This boat exemplifies the "New York model" of 1819*

arrangements became nearly standardized, though there was variation in hull form and appearance.

As a second example, we have a somewhat later and smaller pilot schooner of the same general model (Marestier's example No. 16), shown in Figure 62. Compared with the *Anna Maria,* this schooner is not only smaller but a little deeper in proportion to length. The most marked feature in her design is probably the strong tumble

A NEW YORK PILOT BOAT OF 1800

home amidships. Whether this was a popular fad at the time she was building or whether she was an exception in this respect, cannot be answered since we have so few examples of her contemporaries. As Marestier found her building some time in 1820, she was possibly designed in 1819. I have found two of the original drafts copied by Marestier; they are dated in the period of 1815 to 1819, so it is possible to place a fairly accurate date on our pilot boat. Unfortunately, Marestier did not show any detail, and the deck arrangement had to be restored by reference to the *Anna Maria,* so that her appearance might be better visualized.

This schooner shows another feature of design: the floors are carried well fore and aft, as is indicated by the buttock lines, yet the

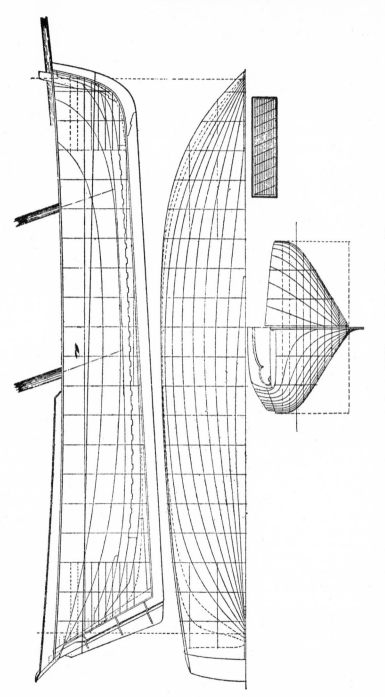

Figure 63. An American pilot schooner of about 1830, probably built at New York. Her midsection seems to be near the mainmast — well aft for that day

ends are quite sharp and reasonably well formed, considering the length of the hull. This gave good capacity yet did not prevent speed unless the hull was too deep and the deadrise insufficient. This principle of design must have increased stability and aided in preventing excessive pitching; it can often be seen in the plans of American schooners of this date. Such schooners as this one and the *Anna Maria,* as well as the pilot schooner of about 1830, Figure 63, illustrate the similarity in looks and model of pilot schooners during the years covered by their dates.

As was pointed out in the chapter on the "Virginia model," the size of pilot schooners was fixed by the demands of their service, and the Sandy Hook schooners were no exception. As their cruising radius increased, so did their size. After 1830 the pilot schooners became larger, for this reason, and became useful for work other than that for which they were intended. Take, for instance, the schooner *Independence.* This large pilot boat was purchased by the U. S. Navy at New York in 1838 and was fitted out as a tender to the larger vessels employed in the famous Wilkes Expedition (sent around the world as an exploring adventure) along with another schooner of the same type, the *Sea Gull.* The *Sea Gull* was lost with all hands off "Cape Stiff," but the *Independence,* under her naval name of *Flying Fish,* went out to the East Indies, where she was sold. Under the name of *Spec* she became a notorious opium clipper and China coaster. Her fascinating history is given in full, along with her portrait, in Lubbock's recent book, *The Opium Clippers.* In passing, it may be mentioned that the *Independence* was unusually large for her type and date, measuring 85'-6" length over all and 22'-6" beam. At least two other pilot schooners were purchased by the Navy before 1853.

Toward the end of the 1830's there was a change in the topside appearance of the Sandy Hook pilot schooners which can best be illustrated by the striking *John McKeon,* built by Isaac Webb in 1838. Built for a company of New Jersey pilots, she seems to have had a short and tragic career, going down with all hands (six men) in the terrible hurricane of July 28th, 1839. It was thought that she was stove in by the fall of her masts. Her lines are presented in

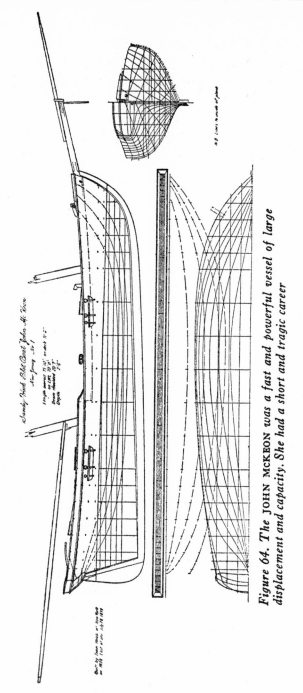

Figure 64. The JOHN McKEON *was a fast and powerful vessel of large displacement and capacity. She had a short and tragic career*

209

Figure 64, and indicate a fast and powerful vessel of large displacement and capacity. Her body is carried well into the ends and the flaring topsides give great stability. It is of interest to note that the *McKeon* had a rockered keel and some hollow in the water lines forward. The big rig of this schooner is shown in Figure 67; the foot of the fore course was spread by a squaresail boom, of course. One of the marked characteristics of the pilot schooners of 1812-1840 seems to have been extremely long lower masts, combined with very short topmasts. The *McKeon* also shows one of the intermediate short steps in the development of the counter from the old transom-counter of early times.

In the '40's there were more changes in the design of pilot boats, brought about by the success of John W. Griffiths' experiments with the very hollow entrance as an intentional feature of design. At first, the pilot boat builders do not seem to have been much impressed, due, perhaps to the fact that they had been using a slight hollow in the entrance for many years, though without bothering to investigate the matter, as Griffiths had done quite thoroughly.

Gradually the hollow entrance became of more interest to the builders and they experimented most conservatively with it. Such a conservative experiment with the Steers-designed *Mary Taylor,* built in 1849. She had somewhat more hollow than had been used previously. This schooner was a great success and attracted wide attention to the principles of her design and to her designer as well. Hence, after 1850, we find the hollow entrance an acknowledged feature in fast schooners.

The rivalry between the various builders of pilot boats and the sporting proclivities of the pilots and their friends made the racing of these boats take on tremendous importance. As a result, there was a continuous search for high speed. Griffiths was now preaching the theory that drag of keel and great deadrise were unnecessary — in fact harmful — in hulls designed for speed. His ideal was a shoal hull with sharp and hollow ends and with little deadrise. In short, the type that he supported was, in the schooner rig, best exemplified in the Essex-built clipper fisherman of the '60's and '70's. Capable

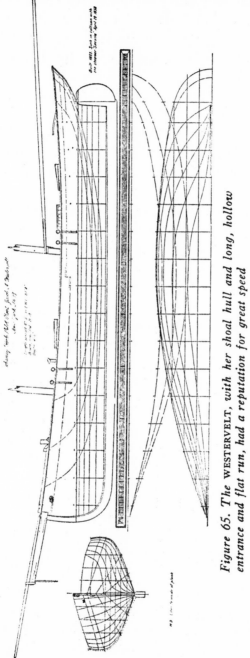

Figure 65. The WESTERVELT, with her shoal hull and long, hollow entrance and flat run, had a reputation for great speed

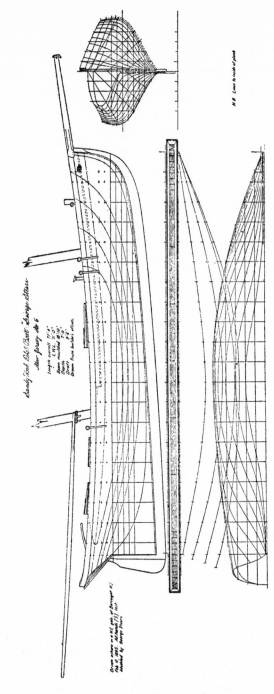

Figure 66. This beautifully modeled schooner, from the board of the noted designer of the famous AMERICA, is an example of George Steers' mature practice

of high speed, this model was the most unsafe that could then be chosen for going to sea in winter.

Nevertheless, pilots adopted the shoal hull and for a few years hulls similar to that of the *Jacob A. Westervelt* (her lines are shown in Figure 65) were popular. The *Westervelt* exhibits many features that later became more or less typical of a large group of pilot schooners. She had the round stern and the exaggerated tumbling in of the stem as well as the low freeboard and strong sheer. The *Westervelt* was built in 1853 and had a big reputation for speed. It is obvious that she would be extraordinarily fast as long as she did not put her rail under, just as was true, later on, with the fast Essex-built clipper fishing schooners.

The long, hollow entrance and the straight, flat run were carried to unusual proportions in this schooner. Such boats carried large rigs, of the common fore and aft type, fitted with fore topmasts. Unlike many of her sisters, the *Westervelt* was not lost through stress of weather but on April 20th, 1858, was run down by the steamer *Saxonia* some 270 miles off the Hook, with the loss of one pilot. The pilots are said to have preferred the shoal schooners to the deep ones because their motion in heavy weather was easier and they were not as wet. This bears out the well-known argumment on behalf of centerboarders for sea work. I have found no record of centerboard schooners being used off the Hook, but the pilots of the southern ports used them with great success.

Returning to George Steers, it is apparent that he did not support the Griffiths theory in regard to drag and deadrise, at least in schooners, for he followed his *Mary Taylor* with the *America*, of more deadrise and drag, then with the two fine pilot schooners, *George Steers* and *Moses H. Grinnell,* along the same general lines as those of the *America*.

The lines of the most workmanlike *George Steers* are shown in Figure 66 as an example of Steers' mature practice. This beautifully modeled schooner is worthy of special attention. I think her run is a slight improvement over that of the *America,* and the balance of her ends is quite remarkable. Her depth is sufficient to insure safety and her midship section is such that a reasonable amount of initial

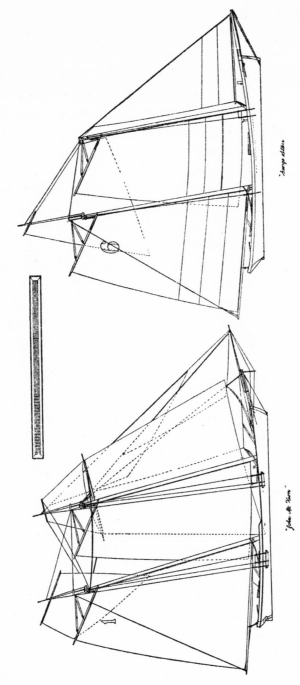

Figure 67. The MCKEON *carried a tremendous rig, with long lower masts and short topmasts. Her odd gaff topsail was characteristic of the period. The* STEERS *is shown with a "baldheaded" rig but with plenty of canvas. Note the club in the head of her "fisherman"*

stability is obtained. The similarity of the *Steers* to the *America* is striking, though the *Steers* is much smaller. This schooner was undoubtedly one of the finest pilot boats ever built, though in later years she would have been considered small.

It is notable that Steers' pilot schooners were not posted as having foundered. The *Grinnell* was cut down by a steamer in 1863, as was the *Taylor,* while the *Steers* went ashore on the Jersey coast near Barnegat in the bad northeast gale of February 12th, 1865, with the loss of all hands (five men). This was the fate of many fine pilot boats when running for shelter during gales from that quarter, while others piled up on Long Island during easterly and southeasterly gales. Truly, the fate of a pilot boat was rarely a happy one; she generally met her end while on station.

From 1855 on, the Sandy Hook pilot schooner became a combination of the ideas expressed in the *Westervelt* and *Steers,* the features of the *Steers* predominating. The close relationship of the Boston and New York boats, after 1855, will enable us to follow the development of the pilot schooners after that year when we discuss the Boston type. The plain and simple rig of the *Steers* is to be seen in Figure 67; it is one that could be used to advantage in small schooners now, did the racing rules allow it. The importance of the pilot schooners can best be illustrated by their influence on yachts. Nearly all schooner yachts until 1870 were on the same general model as the pilot boats, the culmination of that type being the fast *Sappho* and the big *Enchantress.* It may also be said that the influence of the pilot boats on the yachts was a healthy one and it is a pity that it did not last longer.

The end of the sailing pilot boat did not come until the twentieth century, when steamers and auxiliaries of a nondescript character took her place.

Chapter Fifteen

⚓

AMERICAN PILOT BOATS : III

Chapter Fifteen

⚓

AMERICAN PILOT BOATS: III

THE FACT that the abilities of individual designers play a large part in the development of a type of sailing vessel is well illustrated in the case of the Boston pilot schooner. Here was a type that apparently had no great reputation, a mere copy of a model developed elsewhere, which suddenly sprang into prominence when able designers appeared on the scene. In spite of a surprising lack of information regarding the lines and models of early Boston pilot boats, there is a great deal of circumstantial evidence that they were not distinctive in model or fame until well toward the middle of the nineteenth century. As far as has been discovered, the only difference between Boston and New York pilot schooners previous to 1840 was the greater proportionate depth of the former, the Boston boats being more or less exact copies of the New York craft in appearance and rig. Perhaps the Boston builders were less progressive than those of New York, or possibly Boston pilotage was less competitive; at any rate there seems to be no mention of distinctive Boston designs nor is there evidence that Boston boats had any great reputation for speed before 1840. Of course, some fast schooners were built at Boston previous to this time, but it must be inferred that Boston schooners had not the reputation of those found at Norfolk and New York. This inference is borne out, to a marked degree, by the fact that, in the extensive foreign literature on American schooners there was no mention of Boston pilot schooners, though those of New York and Norfolk received special attention because of their reputations.

The designer who probably did most to bring Boston pilot

schooners the great reputation they enjoyed after 1840 was a Dane, Louis (or Lewis) Winde. This man had been educated in Denmark as a naval constructor and had emigrated to Boston sometime before 1836. The reputation of American schooners of the Baltimore clipper type was then very great abroad and Winde seems to have been an enthusiastic follower of the model. The schooner that brought Winde to prominence locally was the Yacht *Northern Light,* built in 1838 for Colonel William P. Winchester. This yacht was 62'-6" long on deck, 17'-6" beam and 7"-3' depth in the hold; she was a remarkably handsome vessel. Her sporting owner soon took the measure of the contemporary pilot and fishing schooners, with the result that the *Northern Light* won a great local reputation. There were other sportsmen in Boston, to whom the supremacy of the Winchester vessel was a source of annoyance; these ordered similar schooners from Winde or went to other designers in search of schooners faster than the *Northern Light.* Among the schooners built for these enthusiastic yachtsmen were the Winde-designed crack *Coquette* which beat the great sloop *Maria* in a match race, the fast *Brenda* by the same designer, and the *Belle,* designed and built by Samuel Hall.

These schooners all became pilot boats after the yachtsmen grew tired of them, the *Coquette* and *Belle* remaining at Boston. The pilots had been busy, in the meantime, with the construction of new schooners of larger size and better models than had been seen before in Boston waters. While the new schooners still retained much of the appearance of the contemporary New York pilot boats, they were much sharper and far deeper. Generally speaking, the Boston schooners were narrower than the New York vessels of the same type. A good example of the new class of Boston pilot schooner appeared in 1840 after the *Frolic,* launched at East Boston in 1843. She was 70 feet on deck, 18'-10" beam, 7'-10" depth of hold and drew 9 feet aft and 6 feet forward. She had but 18 inches of sheer and the quarter deck was 6 inches above the main deck at the great beam. She carried a 66-foot foremast, a 68-foot mainmast, and a bowsprit reaching 13 feet outboard; she tonned 90. The *Belle,* built the year before as a yacht, was 66'-1" on deck, 18'-6" beam, 6'10" depth of hold, 72 tons.

It should be mentioned that the *Frolic* followed New York practice in pilot boat design in that she had a raised quarter deck. This had been a feature of *Northern Light* and *Coquette*. Late in the '40's, flush-decked pilot boats became popular at Boston; though a few such schooners were built at New York from time to time, most of these were not actually built for the pilot service

A BOSTON PILOT BOAT OF 1884

but for trade, even though their lines had been taken from the famous New York pilot boat model. The reason that Boston pilots like the flush-decked schooner while the New Yorkers preferred the raised quarter deck has not been discovered; there was probably a practical reason for the preference, however.

The type of schooner that had been introduced by Winde followed the extreme Baltimore clipper model, having great drag and much rake to the ends. Perhaps the most marked feature of the new Boston boats was their extraordinary rise of floor; their deadrise was much greater than had been generally used in pilot schooners built elsewhere. During the late '40's and early '50's, the Boston pilot schooners became shoaler but never reached the extremes in this direction that have been noticed in the New York boats. Winde's schooners, and the earlier pilot boats, had the broken sheer that had been popular in the New York craft; when flush-decked vessels became popular, flush sheers naturally followed.

Figure 68 shows the lines of an unidentified Boston pilot boat built at East Boston in 1845. She is much shoaler than such schooners as Winde's *Coquette,* following the trend in design that was appearing at the time of her launching. It might be observed that she was an almost complete reversion to the type of Baltimore clipper that had been popular in the slave trade twenty years earlier. The scarcity of models and plans of Boston pilot schooners of her period makes any claim that the example is "typical" of her class extremely doubtful, but she does represent a degree of evolution in the Boston pilot schooner type. Judging by the few lines and models that have been found, the development of the Boston schooners was very rapid between 1842 and 1855. It will be noticed that Figure 68 shows a schooner of the flush-decked type.

Winde's schooners, along with those designed by Joseph Lee and Samuel Hall, had firmly established the reputation of the Boston pilot schooner by 1850, both at home and abroad. About this time another designer appeared whose eccentric genius was to enhance the reputation that the Boston pilot boats had earned through the ability of Winde and his contemporaries. This was Dennison J. Lawlor, born in New Brunswick, who was as remarkable for his designs as he was for personal peculiarities. Temperamental and exacting though he was, Lawlor will long be remembered as the designer of some of the finest pilot boats and fishermen ever seen in New England waters. He was probably the greatest rival of Steers in schooner design, but by the time Steers died Lawlor had outstripped him in experience. Not only had Lawlor designed commercial schooners but he had also turned out yachts, steamers and a number of small brigantines of note. One of the most noted of Lawlor's brigantines was the Mediterranean fruiter *News Boy,* built at Thomaston, Maine, in 1854, a 111-foot vessel of 299 tons.

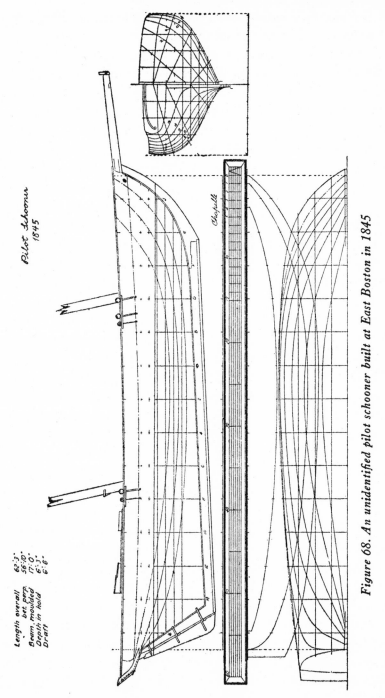

Pilot schooner
1845

Chapelle

Length overall   62'3".
     bet. perp.   56'10".
Beam, moulded   17'0".
Depth in hold   6'3".
Draft   6'6".

Figure 68. An unidentified pilot schooner built at East Boston in 1845

Lawlor's pilot boats are our particular concern, however, so we must return to them. Figure 69 is a reproduction of the lines of one of the early pilot schooners from the board of this remarkable man. This schooner is the *Dancing Feather,* built in 1853; her model is in the Watercraft Collection in the U. S. National Museum, Washington, D. C. The lines do not give a really accurate impression of the beauty of form that is apparent in the model, as is so often the case. This beautiful schooner had black topsides and green underbody, with her billet, headrails and trailboards picked out with gold leaf. Compared to Lawlor's later pilot boats, the *Dancing Feather* was rather shoal but she was considered a fine sea boat; her motion was very easy in heavy weather.

The importance of easy motion is appreciated by yachtsmen who have had the misfortune to be caught out in an uneasy yacht. Pilots attached a great deal of importance to this quality for they had to live on their vessels for long periods and an uneasy vessel would have exhausted them to such an extent that their efficiency would have been impaired. Hence a schooner that did not posssss this quality was soon disposed of.

The *Dancing Feather* had the clipper bow that had become popular in contemporary fishing schooners of the "sharpshooter" class, which undoubtedly added much to her beauty. The clipper bow was more in favor with the Boston pilots than at New York, probably because of the tradition started by the old *Coquette.* Throughout the last portion of the nineteenth century there were clipper-bowed pilot schooners in use around Boston, though the utilitarian straight stem so characteristic of the New York boats was generally most common. The round stern seen in the plan of the *Dancing Feather* seems to have been an importation from New York and enjoyed only a short popularity around Boston. The trunk cabin seen in the plan was used in a number of the smaller Boston boats; the larger boats had flush decks, broken only by companionways and skylights. The rig of the schooners of the *Dancing Feather* type, Figure 70, was similar to that of the "clipper" fishing schooner — fore and main topmasts fidded, and jibboom.

The list of pilot schooners designed by Lawlor during his long

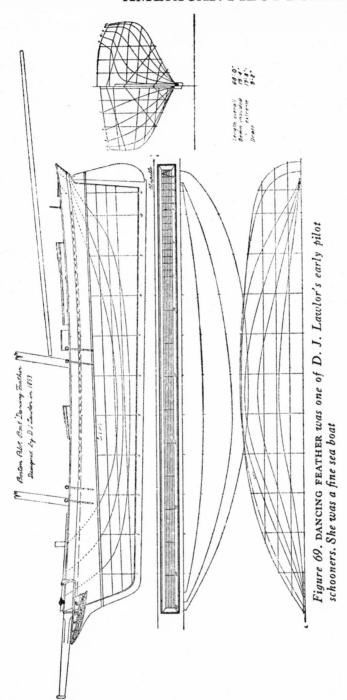

Boston Pilot Boat Dancing Feather
Designed by D J Lawlor in 1853

length overall   68' 0"
beam moulded   19' 4"
Draft extreme   9' 2"

Figure 69. DANCING FEATHER was one of D. J. Lawlor's early pilot schooners. She was a fine sea boat

career is not available at present. There is a good selection of his designs in the six half-models in the Watercraft Collection, including the *Edwin Forrest,* 1865; *Florence,* 1867; the sisters *Phantom* and *Pet,* 1868; *Lillie,* 1876; and the great *Hesper,* built in 1884. Another of his designs was the *D. F. Lawlor,* but her model has not been found. All of the models in the Watercraft Collection

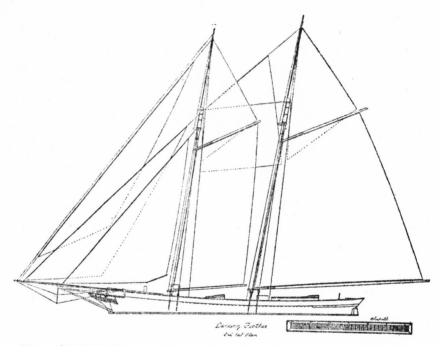

Figure 70. Sail plan of DANCING FEATHER

represent fast schooners, the *Forrest, Lillie* and *Hesper* having the greatest reputations, perhaps. All were straight-stemmers. The *Lillie* was considered the handsomest of the Boston pilot schooners in her time. She had a graceful sheer and a well proportioned rig. The V-shaped transom was used in these schooners in place of the round stern seen in the earlier *Dancing Feather.*

Lawlor's pilot boats, from 1865 on, had sharp, hollow bows and short, though well-formed, runs; the quarter beam buttocks were usually quite straight aft. Lawlor also employed hollow garboards

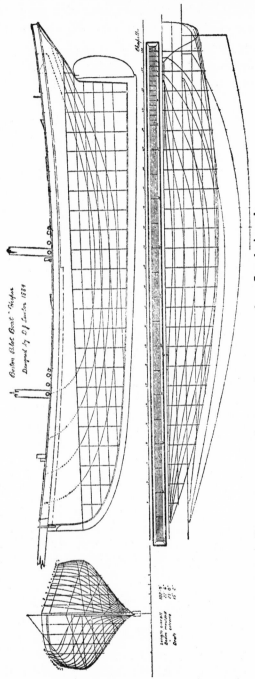

Figure 71. HESPER *was deeper and narrower than Lawlor's other schooners. Her speed and weatherliness were phenomenal*

in most of his designs, usually using very rising floors. Though he retained the drag of the earlier boats, his schooners generally had upright sternposts combined with a rockered stem. There is a slight similarity between his designs and those of Steers, though Lawlor's vessels showed much less rocker on the keel. One characteristic of the Lawlor models is their very thin deadwood at the heel of the sternpost, resulting from their extraordinarily fine water lines aft.

The lines of the best known of all of Lawlor's pilot schooners is shown in Figure 71. This is the *Hesper,* whose speed and weatherliness were phenomenal. The proudest boast of any fisherman or schooner of her time was that she once "beat the *Hesper.*" This was often a matter of an active imagination rather than of fact, for some of the "races" were run off when the crew of the *Hesper* were wholly unaware of the fact that there was a race. Properly handled, the *Hesper* would work to windward better than any of her contemporaries and in a blow she was almost unbeatable.

This pilot schooner was built in 1884 and was a departure from Lawlor's earlier practice. She was much deeper than any of his other schooners, in proportion to beam, and was rather narrow. When she was building, some of the pilots were rather skeptical as to her stability because of these features in her design. To some extent, their skepticism was well founded for the *Hesper* was found to require a little outside ballast, a method of gaining stability that was not regarded with much enthusiasm by the pilots. However, the *Hesper* was so smart a sailer and so able that this fault was forgiven her; for years she was the pride of the Boston pilots.

The *Hesper* was one of the largest schooners that had been built for the pilot service at Boston, measuring about 102 feet over all and 23 feet beam. Most of the earlier schooners were under 80 feet over all. The *Hesper* differed from most of her contemporaries in having a raised quarter deck, though her rail was flush. She was not a particularly handsome vessel, judging by photographs, for she had a high, bold bow which gave her an appearance of great power rather than grace. When she first came out, the *Hesper* had the old-fashioned jibboom but this was replaced with a spike bowsprit shortly after her launch. Photographs of the *Hesper* in dry dock show her to have had much of the appearance of the contemporary English cutter yachts, at least so far as her forebody was concerned. It is quite probable that Lawlor was influenced by the cutter, for it will be remembered that the controversy between the "cutter cranks" and supporters of the "skimming dishes" was then at its height. Boston leaned toward the side of the "cutter cranks" and Lawlor was keenly interested in the matter; he was an advocate of the keel type, it is said.

It was the race against the *Hesper* that made the reputation of the Burgess-designed fisherman *Fredonia*. The *Hesper* was beaten by the *Fredonia* in a strong breeze, with the result that the latter won tremendous fame locally. Moreover, I have been told by yachtsmen who saw this famous race that the pilots did not do justice to the *Hesper*. It seems that the pilots had a balloon jib of which they were inordinately proud; this they tried to carry to windward in the race, with the result that their great schooner sagged off to leeward. Many expert onlookers were of the opinion that had the *Hesper* been properly handled she would have won, though the result would have been a very close race. It must be remembered that the *Hesper* often suffered, during these test races, by having to sail under her working rig while her opponent was generally a new vessel with a new set of sails and carefully tuned up.

The rivalry between the pilot schooners ran very high, and pilots on each vessel were fanatical supporters of their vessel. The *Hesper* had a large "gravy-boat" in her mess service and this was known by the pilot number of her greatest rival, to the great annoyance of the pilots in that schooner. Because of the pride of her pilots, the *Hesper* was sailed very hard, day in and day out, with the result that she is remembered as having been a "workhouse" by many of the pilots who were apprentices in her.

None of the schooners built after the *Hesper* achieved anything like her reputation, though the *America* came nearest to it. The *America* was designed by Thomas F. McManus who is best known for his fishermen. She was built in 1896-97 by Bishop at Gloucester, to the order of Captain James Reid, a well-known Boston pilot. Captain Reid had commanded the yacht *America* during the latter

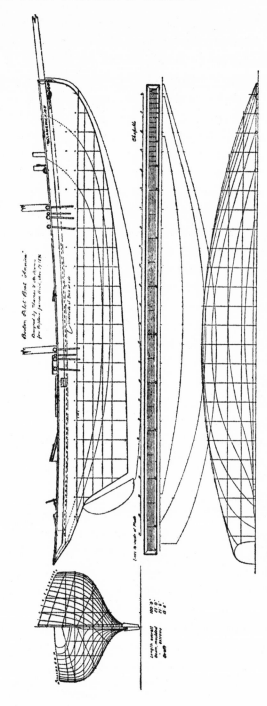

Figure 72. AMERICA had the "Indian head" carried by her designer's fishing schooners. She succeeded HESPER as the Boston "trial horse"

part of that famous vessel's career and he named the new pilot boat in her honor. The *America* was quite different from the *Hesper,* as may be seen by the former's lines, shown in Figure 72. In many respects, the *America* was much like McManus' fishermen, having the "Indian head" and the rather round midship section. The new schooner had a long run, but it was slightly fuller than in McManus' later schooners. The small transom was a distinct departure from previous practice and the fullness of the *America's* quarter beam buttock may be traced to this feature, at least to some extent.

The *America* succeeded the *Hesper* as the Boston "trial horse" and in this capacity sailed against most of the Boston fishing fleet. After many years of service, she was finally sold as a Cape Verde packet. Throughout her career as a pilot boat, the *America* proved herself to be not only fast but a most comfortable sea boat. Some of the Boston pilot boats in addition to the *Hesper,* had outside ballast, among them the *America* and *Columbia.*

Following the success of the fisherman *Fredonia,* the pilots had some schooners designed by Edward Burgess, of which the *Adams,* named for the Essex shipbuilder who laid her down, is the best known. This schooner was a very able boat but never developed much speed, probably because she had a very full run. If there was any severe criticism of either Lawlor's or Burgess' pilot boats, it was the tendency to get the center of buoyancy too far aft. It must be added, however, that this was due largely to the trend of "scientific" yacht design at the time these designers were active. The fullness in the runs of many of the schooners of the '70's and '80's, both yachts and commercial craft, can be traced to the over-enthusiastic acceptance of the pseudo-scientific "wave-line theory" by the leading designers of the period. After the great work of the English yacht designer, Dixon Kemp, became available to designers in this country, it is noticeable that there was a reversion to the better formed runs of earlier times, following Kemp's investigations of the quarter beam buttock. Incidentally, Kemp's theory is carried out in the design of the *Hesper.*

There was one other designer of Boston pilot schooners who was very successful. He was Ambrose A. Martin, a yacht builder, who modeled the schooners *Columbia, George Warren, Louise* and *Liberty*. It was the handsome *Columbia* that lay on Scituate Beach, near the old lighthouse, for so many years. She was embayed during the famous "Portland Breeze" and came ashore there during the height of the storm, all hands being lost. For years she was a landmark, resting on her side, in a good state of preservation; when the new concrete breakwater was built a few years ago, the wreck was removed. The Columbia had a handsome clipper bow and was one of the many Boston pilot schooners built by Bishop, at Gloucester.

Though steam pilot boats have not been employed at Boston, the old sailing vessels have partially disappeared. The last of the old boats is the *Liberty,* recently condemned. A number of yachts have been purchased by the pilots, though this practice is not a recent one, as is evidenced by the case of the *Coquette.* Among the yachts that became Boston pilot boats, the *Tarolinta* and *Fleur de Lys* are best known, though neither was particularly fast. The latter had been a centerboarder, but it is believed that the board was removed when she became a pilot boat. The only Boston pilot boat that was built with a centerboard, and designed for this particular business, was the Burgess-designed *Varuna.* It was hoped that the use of a centerboard would produce a fast vessel, but in this case the pilots seem to have been disappointed for the experiment was never repeated. So far as can be learned, most of the centerboard pilot schooners were built for southern ports.

A large number of Boston pilot schooners were built for other ports; some went to China in the '40's, and more recently one or two went to the West Coast. The day of the sailing pilot boat is now over, however, for the few that are left in service have their rigs so cut down that they are but "motor sailers," with the emphasis on "motor." The types of boats used in the past are of interest, at this time, for they offer suggestions for an excellent type of seagoing auxiliary cruiser. If reports are to be relied upon, some of our modern ocean racers are far less comfortable than these old schooners, so perhaps something can still be learned from them.

INDEX

INDEX

INDEX

INDEX